Each today
well lived
makes yesterday
a dream of
happiness
and
each tomorrow
a vision of hope.
Look therefore
to this one day,
for it alone is life.

Cross Stitch
Wit & Wisdom

Over 45 designs with words to brighten your day

Joan Elliott

David and Charles

To Alexander and James,
may your love of the written word
always take you to special places

A DAVID & CHARLES BOOK
Copyright © David & Charles Limited 2007

David & Charles is an F+W Publications Inc. company
4700 East Galbraith Road
Cincinnati, OH 45236

First published in the UK in 2007
First paperback edition 2007

Photography and layout copyright © David & Charles 2007
Text, designs and decorative artwork copyright © Joan Elliott 2007

Joan Elliott has asserted her right to be identified as author of this work
in accordance with the Copyright, Designs and Patents Act, 1988.

A catalogue record for this book is available from the British Library.

ISBN-13: 978-0-7153-2476-9 hardback
ISBN-10: 0-7153-2476-4 hardback

ISBN-13: 978-0-7153-2477-6 paperback
ISBN-10: 0-7153-2477-2 paperback

Printed in China by SNP Leefung
for David & Charles
Brunel House   Newton Abbot   Devon

Executive Editor Cheryl Brown
Editor Jennifer Fox-Proverbs
Desk Editor Bethany Dymond
Art Editor Prudence Rogers
Senior Designer Charly Bailey
Project Editor and chart preparation Lin Clements
Photography Kim Sayer and Michael Crocker
Production Controller Ros Napper

Visit our website at www.davidandcharles.co.uk

David & Charles books are available from all good bookshops; alternatively you can contact our
Orderline on 0870 9908222 or write to us at FREEPOST EX2 110, D&C Direct, Newton Abbot, TQ12 4ZZ
(no stamp required UK only); US customers call 800-289-0963 and Canadian customers
call 800-840-5220.

Contents

Introduction

Words are truly the voice of the heart. For centuries, the joys, sorrows and wisdom of the human spirit have been written, spoken, sung, and yes, stitched in words. Early counted thread work samplers not only reflected the skills of a child's hand but also expressed pride in their achievement. These kept records of family births and deaths and displayed words of faith, hope and love.

Through words, wisdom is passed from old to young in hopes that lessons learned will light the way for the next generation. Through the language of wit and humour, life's burdens can be eased and new possibilities can be seen. Surely there is nothing like being able to laugh at ourselves to give us some perspective!

The chapters of this book are filled with projects that will inspire, amuse and celebrate your life. For the spirit, an Eastern Promise sampler speaks of joy and the promise of hope. For the family, there are gifts to stitch for the newest arrival as well as for parents, grandparents and siblings. A special tribute to teenagers points out all the things that make them so lovable. The family cat is also featured; showing us just what it is that makes cats so special.

To celebrate lasting love there is a delicate sampler made up into a lovely keepsake album, where your favourite couple can hold shared memories. For a more humorous look at relationships, stitch up some 'Meditations on Life' so you can post a few words of wisdom with a feminine point of view. You will also find a special section for gardeners, a subject near and dear to my heart. The holidays are here too: gift bags, ornaments and banners celebrate of the joys of the season.

No matter which words you choose to stitch from this collection of wit and wisdom, I do hope that they will give expression to your thoughts and bring joy to your heart.

Meditations on Life

These days it seems our coping skills are regularly put to the test but don't despair! These wise women have some advice to summon the womanly strength and perseverance that lies within us. Enjoy some quiet time, sit back and relax with a cup of coffee and let your other half sleep in. Rely on your sixth sense when that invisible wall blocks communication. Let people know that they'll have to wait in line while you take care of yourself. Finally, when the mind is willing but the body is protesting, take comfort in knowing that 'this too shall pass'. These four fun notices will help you through the daily stresses with a wink of humour and a nod to the true wisdom that all women possess.

Meditation Pictures

Stitch count (each picture)
98h x 70w

Design size (each picture)
18 x 12.7cm (7 x 5in)

Materials (each picture)
30.5 x 25.5cm (12 x 10in) antique white 14-count Aida

Tapestry needle size 24

DMC stranded cotton (floss) as listed in chart key

1 Prepare for work, referring to page 101 if necessary. Find and mark the centre of the fabric and the centre of the relevant chart on pages 8–14. Mount your fabric in an embroidery frame if you wish.

2 Start stitching from the centre of the chart, using two strands of stranded cotton (floss) for cross stitches. Following the chart for colour changes, work all French knots using one strand wrapped twice around the needle and then work all backstitches using one strand.

3 Once all the stitching is complete, finish your picture by mounting and framing (see page 103 for advice).

Have you noticed that well-behaved women rarely make history?

Wake Up Grumpy
DMC stranded cotton

Cross stitch

▨	208
◪	209
▨	210
◉	310
▨	317
Y	318
▨	334
▨	349
▥	351
▨	352
▨	415
▨	725
o	726
▨	727
H	729
▨	869
▨	905
✕	906
▨	907
\	945
▨	951
▨	961
V	962
T	3716
▨	3755
▨	3829
–	3841
•	blanc

Backstitch
—— 310

French knots
● 310
◌ 725

I'm Still Hot!
DMC stranded cotton
Cross stitch

▦	208
╱	209
▨	210
⊙	310
▨	317
Y	318
▨	349
▮	351
▨	352
▨	415
+	676
▨	725
o	726
▨	727
⌶	729
▨	905
✕	906
▨	907
╲	945
▨	951
▦	961
V	962
▨	3755
▨	3829
−	3841
•	blanc

Backstitch
——— 310

French knots
● 208
● 310
○ blanc

Shout!
DMC stranded cotton
Cross stitch

◨	310
	317
Y	318
	334
	415
+	676
	725
I	729
	869
	905
×	906
	907
\	945
	951
	961
V	962
	3716
	3755
	3829
−	3841
•	blanc

Backstitch
—— 310
—— 349
—— 905

French knots
● 310
● 349

I can only please one person a day. Today is not your day.

and tomorrow is not looking good.

For the Love of Cats

This chapter has a selection of fun feline-inspired designs for cat lovers everywhere. There are many words to describe a cat – independent, intelligent, playful – but no matter how we characterize them, cats have earned a special place in our hearts, living up to the sentiment, 'A house is not a home without a cat'. After all, a warm day is purr-fect for a pampered feline to lounge by a cottage window. What could be more like a cat than a peaceful afternoon nap? Keep the house quiet with a charming door plate while you treat yourself to some relaxation. An easy-to-stitch paw prints frame allows you to proudly display your best kitty photo. For a taste of luxury, stitch up a little 'cat-titude', complete with gold-beaded crown and jewels, mounting the design into a wooden jewellery box or a card for your favourite cat lover.

Cottage Cat Picture

Stitch count
155h x 111w

Design size
28 x 20cm (11 x 8in)

Materials
40.6 x 33cm (16 x 13in) antique white 14-count Aida

Tapestry needle size 24

DMC stranded cotton (floss) as listed in chart key

1 Prepare for work, referring to page 101 if necessary. Mark the centre of the fabric and centre of the chart on pages 24–25. Mount your fabric in an embroidery frame if you wish.

2 Start stitching from the centre of the chart and fabric, using two strands of stranded cotton (floss) for full and three-quarter cross stitches. Work all French knots using two strands wound once around the needle. Following the chart colours, use one strand for all backstitches and for the long stitches in the flower stems and lettering.

3 Once all the stitching is complete, finish your picture by mounting and framing (see page 103).

Women and cats will do as they please – men and dogs should relax and get used to it!

16

A house is not
a home
without a Cat!

Cat Nap Door Plate

Who would be able to disturb this sweet snoozing pussy cat? Hang this easy-to-make sign and keep your afternoon nap free of disturbances.

Stitch count
57h x 73w

Design size
10.3 x 13.2cm (4 x 5¼in)

Materials

23 x 25.5cm (9 x 10in) antique white 14-count Aida

Tapestry needle size 24

DMC stranded cotton (floss) as listed in chart key

11.5 x 15.2cm (4½ x 6in) heavy white card

Two pieces 16.5 x 20.3cm (6½ x 8in) of felt to tone with embroidery

Lightweight iron-on interfacing and fusible web

0.5m (½yd) length of 6mm (¼in) wide ribbon to tone with embroidery

Permanent fabric glue

Three decorative satin roses

*Cats are the connoisseurs of comfort.
(James Herriot)*

1 Prepare for work, referring to page 101 if necessary. Mark the centre of the fabric and centre of the chart on page 23. Mount fabric in an embroidery frame if you wish.

2 Start stitching from the centre of the chart and fabric, using two strands of stranded cotton (floss) for full and three-quarter cross stitches. Work all French knots using two strands wound once around the needle. Following the chart colours, use one strand for backstitches and for the long stitches in the whiskers.

3 Once all the stitching is complete, make up into a door plate as follows. Cut a piece of iron-on interfacing 2.5cm (1in) larger than the finished embroidery all around. With the wrong side of your work facing, centre the interfacing and fuse to the embroidery. Trim the embroidery ten rows beyond the design. Fold the edges to the back leaving a three-row border all around. Press the folds. Trim the heavy card to

fit behind the embroidery under the folded edges. Glue the folded edges to the back of the card with permanent fabric glue.

4 Cut a piece of fusible web to match the felt size and sandwich between the two pieces of felt. Using a press cloth, iron to fuse the layers, leaving the top long edge open. For a decorative effect, use pinking shears all around the felt close to the edge. Cut the length of ribbon in half and position the two lengths 4cm (1½in) from either side of the felt, inserting it 2.5cm (1in) between the layers. Iron to fuse the top edge.

5 Apply permanent fabric glue sparingly to the back of the embroidery close to the edge. Carefully position the embroidery on the felt leaving an equal border all around. Press down to fix in place, but make sure no glue oozes out. Add decorative roses at bottom centre and where the ribbon meets the top edge. To finish, tie the ribbons in a bow to create a hanger.

Paw Prints Frame

This cheerful photo frame is great for displaying a picture of your favourite feline, or you could insert a small mirror instead.

Stitch count
113h x 85w

Design size
20.5 x 15.5cm (8 x 6in)

Materials
20 x 28cm (8 x 11in) sheet of clear
14-count plastic canvas

Tapestry needle size 24

DMC stranded cotton (floss)
as listed in chart key

21 x 16cm (8¼ x 6¼in)
heavy white card

21 x 16cm (8¼ x 6¼in) white
foamcore mounting board

Double-sided adhesive tape

1 Prepare the canvas sheet by trimming any rough edges. Mark the centre of the canvas and centre of the chart on page 22.

2 Start stitching from the centre of the chart and canvas, using two strands of stranded cotton (floss) for cross stitches and one strand for all backstitches.

3 Once stitching is complete, make up into a frame, as follows. Leaving one row of plastic

canvas all around, trim the canvas along the outside edge of the embroidery and along the inner edge of the centre rectangle.

4 Attach your photo to the centre of the white card with double-sided tape. Apply more tape close to the outside edges of the card. Place the embroidery on top, with edges flush. Now apply tape close to the edges of the mounting board and place the embroidery on top, with edges flush.

Plastic canvas is pliable and easy to trim, especially if you use sharp-pointed scissors.

Cat-titude Jewellery Box

This fun cat design, embellished with shiny metallic thread and gold beads, is perfect to adorn a jewellery box lid.

Stitch count
65h x 65w

Design size
11.8 x 11.8cm (4½ x 4½in)

Materials

24 x 24cm (9½ x 9½in) light blue 14-count Aida

Tapestry needle size 24 and a beading needle

DMC stranded cotton (floss) as listed in chart key

Kreinik #8 Fine Braid: 028 citron

Mill Hill Magnifica beads: 10076 gold

Simply Square wooden box (see Suppliers)

1 Prepare for work, referring to page 101 if necessary. Mark the centre of the fabric and centre of the chart on page 23. Mount fabric in an embroidery frame if you wish.

2 Start stitching from the centre of the chart and fabric, using two strands of stranded cotton (floss) for full and three-quarter cross stitches. Work all French knots using two strands wound once around the needle. Following the chart colours, use one strand for backstitches but two strands of DMC 349 for backstitching the sunglasses. Use one strand for the long stitches in the whiskers and lettering. Use one strand of Kreinik thread to long stitch the stars. Using a beading needle and matching thread, attach the beads (see page 102).

3 Once all the stitching is complete, mount your embroidery in the wooden box according to the manufacturer's instructions.

Cat-titude Card

Stitch count 65h x 65w
Design size 9.2 x 9.2cm (3½ x 3½in)

Work the design on 21.6cm (8½in) square of light blue 18-count Aida. Use the threads listed in the key on page 23. Replace Mill Hill Magnifica beads with petite glass beads 40557 gold and replace the Kreinik #8 braid 028 citron braid with finer Kreinik #4 braid 028 citron. Follow the stitching instructions for the jewellery box above. Mount your embroidery in a suitable card (see page 102) and embellish as desired.

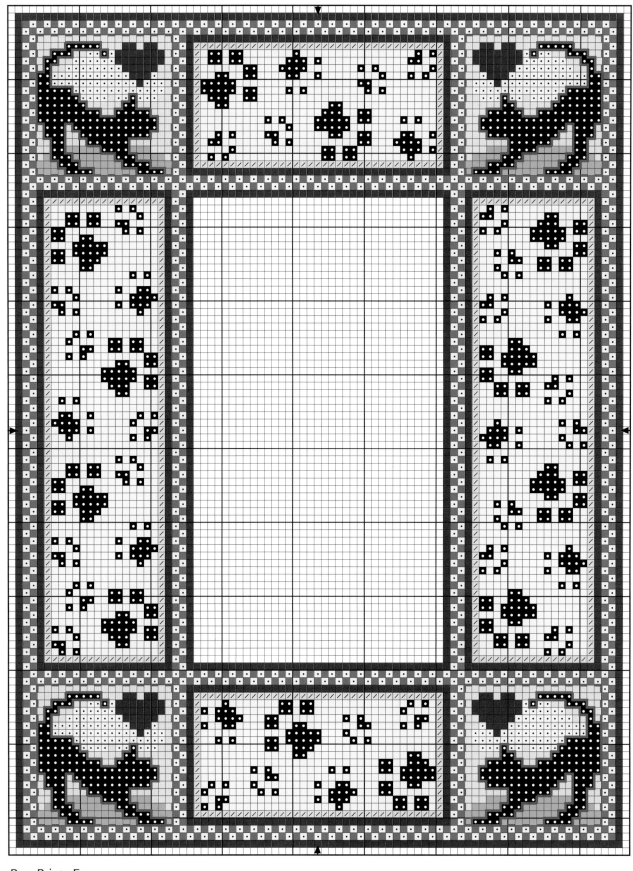

Paw Prints Frame
DMC stranded cotton

Cross stitch

- ■ 310
- ■ 322
- ■ 349
- ⁄ 745
- ☐ 746
- ☐ 907
- ▨ 3841
- • blanc

Backstitch

- — 310

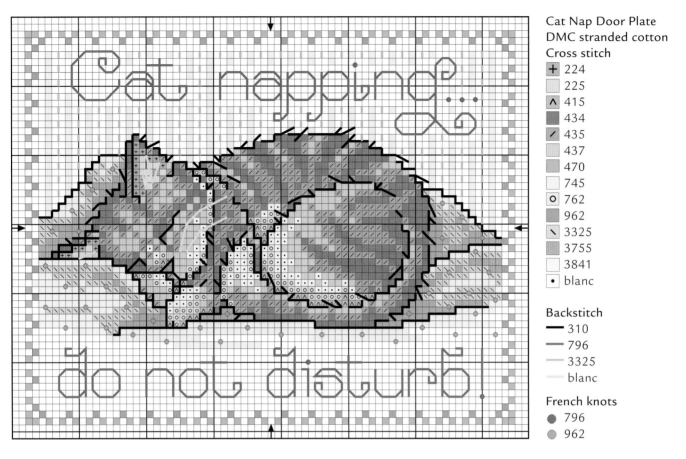

Cat Nap Door Plate
DMC stranded cotton
Cross stitch

+	224
	225
∧	415
	434
∕	435
	437
	470
	745
○	762
	962
╲	3325
	3755
	3841
•	blanc

Backstitch

▬	310
▬	796
▪▪▪	3325
▬	blanc

French knots

●	796
●	962

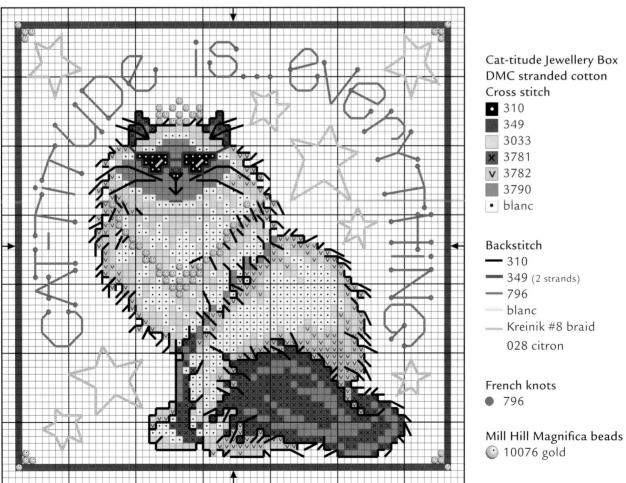

Cat-titude Jewellery Box
DMC stranded cotton
Cross stitch

▨	310
	349
	3033
✕	3781
∨	3782
	3790
•	blanc

Backstitch

▬	310
▬	349 (2 strands)
▬	796
▬	blanc
▬	Kreinik #8 braid
	028 citron

French knots

●	796

Mill Hill Magnifica beads

◓	10076 gold

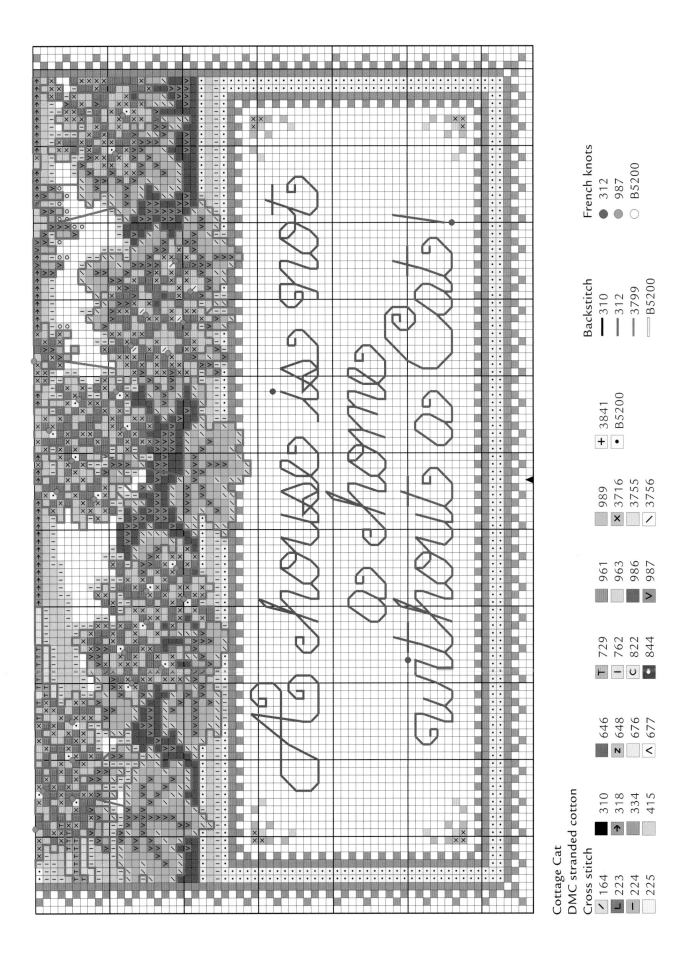

A house is not a home without a Cat!

Cottage Cat

DMC stranded cotton

Cross stitch

	164		646		729		961		989
■	310	N	648	I	762		963	X	3716
↑	318		676	C	822		986		3755
I	224		677	◆	844	V	987	／	3756
	225								

+	3841
•	B5200

Backstitch

——	310
——	312
——	3799
——	B5200

French knots

●	312
●	987
○	B5200

Chinese Proverbs

Asian culture abounds with ancient wisdom. Chinese proverbs provide the inspiration for this chapter to bring us words of hope and beauty as we journey through life. There are four beautiful designs to choose from. The proverbs pictures, photographed overleaf, are to be displayed as a pair. In the first design, butterflies dance amongst golden chrysanthemums, the delicate creatures signifying love, and the late-blooming flowers, a symbol of wisdom. In the second picture, a resplendent bird sits gracefully on a branch of apricot blossoms singing a song of courage and hope.

A photo album (opposite) is an ideal gift for someone starting a new chapter in life or returning from a long journey, reminding them that each step forward leads to the next. When someone dear to you needs encouragement, a handmade card can mean a great deal. The brilliant leaves of the red maple and a sparkling brocade border frame words to awaken the spirit and express your support for whatever path they wish to take.

Proverbs Pictures

Stitch count (each picture)
99h x 71w

Design size (each picture)
18 x 12.8cm (7 x 5in)

Materials (each picture)
30.5 x 25.5cm (12 x 10in) 28-count white Monaco evenweave
✿
Tapestry needle size 24 and a beading needle
✿
DMC stranded cotton (floss) as listed in chart key
✿
Kreinik #4 Very Fine Braid: 028 citron
✿
Mill Hill antique glass beads: 03021 royal pearl
(for Bird and Blossom picture)
✿
Mill Hill glass seed beads: 00374 rainbow (for Butterflies and Chrysanthemum picture)

1 Prepare for work, referring to page 101 if necessary. Mark the centre of the fabric and centre of the chart on page 34 or 35. Mount your fabric in an embroidery frame if you wish.

2 Start stitching from the centre of the chart and fabric, working over two fabric threads. Use one strand for Kreinik thread cross stitches. Use two strands of stranded cotton (floss) for all other full and three-quarter cross stitches. Work all DMC French knots using two strands wound once around the needle. Work all Kreinik French knots using one strand. Following the chart colours, use one strand for all backstitches. Using a beading needle and matching thread, attach the beads (see page 102).

3 Once all stitching is complete, finish your picture by mounting and framing (see page 103).

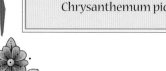

Chinese Temple Album

Covered in suede and highlighted with golden threads this small photo album makes a thoughtful and lasting gift.

Stitch count
69h x 69w

Design size
9.7 x 9.7cm (3¾ x 3¾in)

Materials

23 x 23cm (9 x 9in) white
18-count Aida

Tapestry needle size 24

DMC stranded cotton (floss)
as listed in chart key

Kreinik #4 Very Fine Braid:
028 citron

23 x 50.8cm (9 x 20in) piece
of Ultrasuede® to tone with
embroidery

Lightweight iron-on interfacing

12.7 x 12.7cm (5 x 5in)
heavy white card

0.5m (½yd) length of black
decorative cord

One small decorative button

Permanent fabric glue

38cm (15in) length of 6mm (¼in)
wide black ribbon

One small album to hold 10 x 15cm
(4 x 6in) photos

1 Prepare for work, referring to page 101. Mark the centre of the fabric and centre of the chart on page 32. Mount your fabric in an embroidery frame if you wish.

2 Start stitching from the centre of the chart and fabric. Use one strand for all Kreinik cross stitches. Use two strands of stranded cotton (floss) for all other cross stitches. Use one strand for all backstitches.

3 Once all the stitching is complete, make up into a slipcase for the photo album. Fold the Ultrasuede® in half lengthways and press to crease. Lay the fabric flat with the album open on top and fold the top and bottom edges in to match the top and bottom edges of the album. Press the folds

in place. Centre the open album on the fabric and fold in the sides to fit, making sure the album closes easily. Press the folds in place. Open up the fabric and carefully glue the top and bottom folds up to where the sides fold in, leaving the pockets free for the album cover to be inserted. Insert the album into the side pockets. When the fit is correct glue the sides in place against the inner edges, top and bottom.

4 Cut iron-on interfacing 2.5cm (1in) larger than the embroidery all around. With the wrong side facing, centre the interfacing and fuse to the embroidery. Trim to ten rows beyond the design. Fold the edges to the back leaving a three-row border all around. Press the folds. Trim the heavy card to fit behind the embroidery under the folded edges. Glue the edges to the back of the card with permanent fabric glue. Press the folds.

5 Stick the embroidery on the front of the cover with permanent fabric glue carefully applied to the back, close to the edges. Starting and ending at centre bottom, attach the cord all around, adding a button where the ends meet. Cut the ribbon in half. At the inside centre of the front and back edge, attach the ribbon by turning over 1.25cm (½in) and gluing in place.

Chinese Maple Card

This elegant card with its bright maple leaves and stylish design would be suitable for a wide variety of occasions.

Stitch count
67h x 67w

Design size
9.5 x 9.5cm (3¾ x 3¾in)

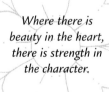

Materials
23 x 23cm (9 x 9in) white 18-count Aida

Tapestry needle size 24

DMC stranded cotton (floss) as listed in chart key

Kreinik #4 Very Fine Braid: 028 citron

Suitable card mount (see Suppliers)

1 Prepare for work, referring to page 101 if necessary. Mark the centre of the fabric and centre of the chart on page 33. Mount fabric in an embroidery frame if you wish.

2 Start stitching from the centre of the chart and fabric. Use one strand for all Kreinik cross stitches. Use two strands of stranded cotton (floss) for all other full and three-quarter cross stitches. Work all DMC French knots using two strands wound once around the needle. Use one strand for working all backstitches.

3 Once all stitching is complete, mount your embroidery in a suitable card and embellish with some gold cord and a decorative button if desired (see page 102 and also suggestions for decorating card mounts).

Where there is beauty in the heart, there is strength in the character.

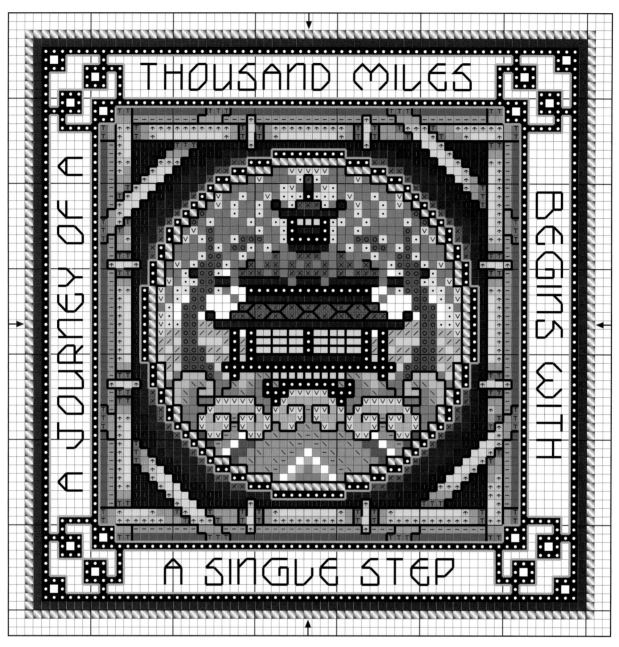

Chinese Temple Album
DMC stranded cotton
Cross stitch

■ 310	✕ 351	↑ 676	▨ 3755	ⱽ 3841
■ 312	▨ 352	▨ 677	• 3756	◰ Kreinik #4 braid
■ 321	▨ 469	▨ 729	⊘ 3787	028 citron
– 322	⁄ 471	⟍ 992	▨ 3814	(1 strand)
■ 349	▨ 472	▨ 993	T 3829	

Backstitch

— 310

⊶ Kreinik #4 braid 028
citron (1 strand)

Chinese Maple Card
DMC stranded cotton

Cross stitch

◎ 300	349	471	• 3756
▪ 310	╱ 351	+ 472	╲ 3841
312	352	3755	▨ Kreinik #4 braid
			028 citron (1 strand)

Backstitch

— 300
— 310
— Kreinik #4 braid
   028 citron (1 strand)

French knots

● 310

Butterflies and
Chrysanthemum
DMC stranded cotton
Cross stitch

▨	310
▨	312
/	334
V	340
T	341
▨	350
O	352
X	471
▨	472
\	677
▨	964
▨	992
+	993
−	3013
L	3746
▨	3755
I	3821
▨	3822
▨	3829
▨	3852
•	blanc
▨	Kreinik #4 braid
	028 citron
	(1 strand)

Backstitch
——	310
——	936
▨	Kreinik #4 braid
	028 citron
	(1 strand)

French knots
● 310

Mill Hill beads
◉ 00374 rainbow

Bird and Blossom

DMC stranded cotton

Cross stitch

310	
312	
334	
340	
341	
351	
352	
471	
472	
677	
936	
975	
976	
992	
993	
3013	
3746	
3755	
3814	
3821	
3822	
3826	
3829	
3852	
blanc	

Kreinik #4 braid
028 citron
(1 strand)

Backstitch

— 310
— 936
— 975
— Kreinik #4 braid
028 citron
(1 strand)

French knots

● 310
◉ Kreinik #4 braid
028 citron
(1 strand)

Mill Hill beads

◉ 03021 royal pearl

Teen Angels

Ah, the joys of raising a teenager. With all their little quirks and habits our young darlings challenge us to see the world through their eyes. But no matter what, let's have our love and support shine through, starting with a list of the top ten things that make teenagers near and dear to our hearts. Make up this cheerful banner as a reminder to your teen that you do see their finer qualities. To echo the theme of this main design I've worked two spin-off projects. For a boy there is a 'totally cool' CD holder for all his favourite music. For a teen princess it's a colourful bag for her next shopping spree. Delivered with a smile and a hug, they are all sure to please.

Ten Things I Love About You Banner

Stitch count
323h x 113w

Design size
58.6 x 20cm (23 x 8in)

Materials
71 x 33cm (28 x 13in) Fiddler's
Light 14-count Aida

Tapestry needle size 24

DMC stranded cotton (floss)
as listed in chart key

0.25m (¼yd) lightweight
iron-on interfacing

0.5m (½yd) background fabric

0.5m (½yd) fusible fleece

0.25m (¼yd) fusible web

1.8m (2yd) decorative trim
to tone with embroidery

Four decorative buttons

Permanent fabric glue

33cm (13in) dowel painted
to tone with embroidery

1 Prepare for work, referring to page 101 if necessary. Mark the centre of the fabric and centre of the chart on pages 44–47. Mount your fabric in an embroidery frame if you wish.

2 Start stitching from the centre of the chart and fabric, using two strands of stranded cotton (floss) for full and three-quarter cross stitches. Work all French knots using two strands wound once around the needle. Following the chart colours, use one strand for backstitches and long stitches. Change the name on the banner using the backstitch alphabet charted on page 42. (Instructions continued overleaf.)

3 Once all the stitching is complete make up as a banner as follows. Cut a piece of iron-on interfacing 2.5cm (1in) larger than the finished embroidery all around. With the wrong side of your work facing, centre the interfacing and fuse it to the embroidery. Now trim the embroidery seven rows beyond the design.

4 Now cut two 68.5 x 33cm (27 x 13in) pieces of background fabric plus three 15 x 10cm (6 x 4in) pieces of fabric for hanging tabs. Cut a 68.5 x 33cm (27 x 13in) piece of fusible fleece and fuse this to the wrong side of one of the fabric pieces following the manufacturer's instructions.

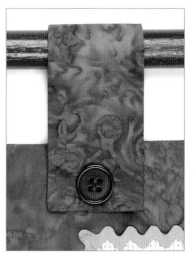

5 To make the tabs, fold each piece of 15 x 10cm (6 x 4in) fabric in half lengthwise, right sides together. Sew a 1.25cm (½in) seam down the length and across one short end. Trim the seam, turn right side out and press. Place the two pieces of background fabric with right sides

facing and pin the tabs evenly across the top of the banner with sewn ends pointing towards the centre and with raw edges matching. Stitch a 1.25cm (½in) seam all around leaving a gap at the bottom for turning. Turn right side out and press. Slipstitch the gap closed.

6 Cut a piece of fusible web to the same size as the prepared embroidery. On the fleece-backed side of the banner, centre the embroidery with the fusible web carefully placed behind it. Fuse according to the manufacturer's instructions. Glue the length of decorative trim carefully to the raw edge of the embroidery, starting and ending at centre bottom, sewing on one of the buttons where the ends meet.

7 Bring the loose ends of the tabs to the front and attach to the banner by sewing on a decorative button. Finally, insert the dowel through the tabs, ready to hang the banner.

There's nothing wrong with teenagers that reasoning with them won't aggravate.

Cool Teen CD Holder

Music and teenagers go hand in hand, so what could be more useful for the teen in your life than this fun CD holder.

Stitch count
63h x 57w

Design size
11.4 x 10.3cm (4½ x 4in)

Materials
25.5 x 23cm (10 x 9in) Fiddler's Light 14-count Aida

Tapestry needle size 24

DMC stranded cotton (floss) as listed in chart key

Lightweight iron-on interfacing

56cm (22in) decorative trim to tone with embroidery

Permanent fabric glue

One decorative button

One standard size CD case

1 Prepare for work, referring to page 101 if necessary. Mark the centre of the fabric and centre of the chart on page 42. Mount fabric in an embroidery frame if you wish.

2 Start stitching from the centre of the chart and fabric, using two strands of stranded cotton (floss) for full and three-quarter cross stitches. Work all French knots using two strands wound once around the needle. Use one strand for all backstitches and long stitches.

3 Once all the stitching is complete, make up into a CD case as follows. Cut a piece of iron-on interfacing 2.5cm (1in) larger than the finished embroidery all around. With the wrong side of your work facing, centre the interfacing and fuse it to the embroidery. Trim the embroidery ten rows beyond the design. Fold the edges to the back leaving a three-row border all around and then press the folds.

4 To attach the embroidery to the CD case, carefully apply glue close to the folded edges on the wrong side and centre the prepared embroidery on the CD case. Glue the length of decorative trim to the folded edge of the embroidery, starting and ending at centre bottom, gluing on the button where the ends meet.

Teen Princess Bag

This brightly coloured bag is very easy to stitch and make up and perfect for a teen princess to carry all her daily essentials in.

Stitch count
69h x 59w

Design size
12.5 x 10.7cm (5 x 4¼in)

Materials
25.5 x 23cm (10 x 9in) Fiddler's Light 14-count Aida

❀

Tapestry needle size 24

❀

DMC stranded cotton (floss) as listed in chart key

❀

Lightweight iron-on interfacing

❀

Ultrasuede® pieces: 23 x 18cm (9 x 7in) for bag front and 30.5 x 18cm (12 x 7in) for bag back

❀

Fusible web

❀

1m (1yd) decorative trim to tone with embroidery

❀

One small and one large decorative button

❀

1m (1yd) decorative cord to tone with trim

❀

Contrasting sewing thread

❀

Permanent fabric glue

❀

One 5cm (2in) piece of Velcro for closing

1 Prepare for work, referring to page 101 if necessary. Mark the centre of the fabric and centre of the chart on page 43. Mount fabric in an embroidery frame if you wish.

2 Start stitching from the centre of the chart and fabric, using two strands of stranded cotton (floss) for full and three-quarter cross stitches. Work all French knots using two strands wound once around the needle. Use one strand for all backstitches and long stitches.

3 Once all the stitching is complete, make up a bag as follows. Cut a piece of iron-on interfacing 2.5cm (1in) larger than the finished embroidery all around. With the wrong side of your work facing, centre the interfacing and fuse it to the embroidery. Trim the embroidery four rows beyond the outer edge of the design.

4 Place the bag front and back pieces of Ultrasuede® together vertically, matching the bottom and side edges. With contrasting thread, stitch a 1.25cm (½in) seam across the bottom and up the two sides, leaving the top edge free. This will leave a 6.4cm (2½in) piece of fabric free at top for the closing flap. Pink all four sides close to the edge. Turn the top flap to the front and press.

5 Cut a piece of fusible web to the same size as the prepared embroidery. On the front of the bag, with the top flap closed, centre the embroidery with the fusible web carefully placed behind it. Fuse together according to the manufacturer's instructions.

6 Glue the length of decorative trim to the raw edge of the embroidery, starting and ending at centre bottom, sewing on the small button where the ends meet. Now glue a length of decorative trim across the bottom of the closing flap 1.25cm (½in) above the pinked edge, folding it over to the back side of the flap and finishing at the centre. Sew the large button on at the front centre of the flap.

7 To attach a carrying cord, open the top flap and glue the length of decorative cord along the inside fold on the back piece of fabric. Attach the Velcro under the centre bottom of the flap and the centre top of the front of the bag to close.

You could make the bag with colourful felt and have fun decorating it with creative trims and buttons.

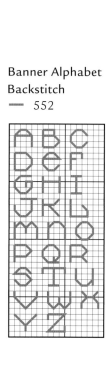

Banner Alphabet
Backstitch
— 552

Cool Teen
DMC stranded cotton

Cross stitch

■ 310	414	✗ 726	■ 817	◉ 938	• blanc
— 312	415	╲ 729	869	○ 945	
T 318	605	742	905	951	
334	676	747	╱ 906	∨ 3755	
350	725	✚ 801	907	3829	

Backstitch
— 310
— 311

French knots
● 310
● 311

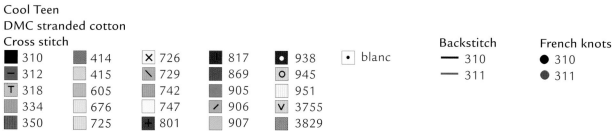

42 Teen Angels

Teen Princess
DMC stranded cotton
Cross stitch

■ 310	▨ 414	▨ 602	◣ 729	▨ 905	ⱽ 3755		Backstitch
– 312	▨ 415	⌊ 603	╱ 742	▨ 906	▨ 3829		— 310
⊤ 318	▨ 552	605	747	▨ 907	Y 3841		— 311
334	< 553	725	◪ 817	○ 945	• blanc		— 817
▨ 350	554	✕ 726	▨ 869	951			

French knots
● 310
● 311
● 350

Backstitch
—— 310
—— 311
—— 552
—— 817

French knots
● 310
● 311
● 350
○ 725

Change the
name using
the alphabet
on page 42

your
a gourmet
taste

your
fashion
sense

your
capacity
to stay calm

your
ability to

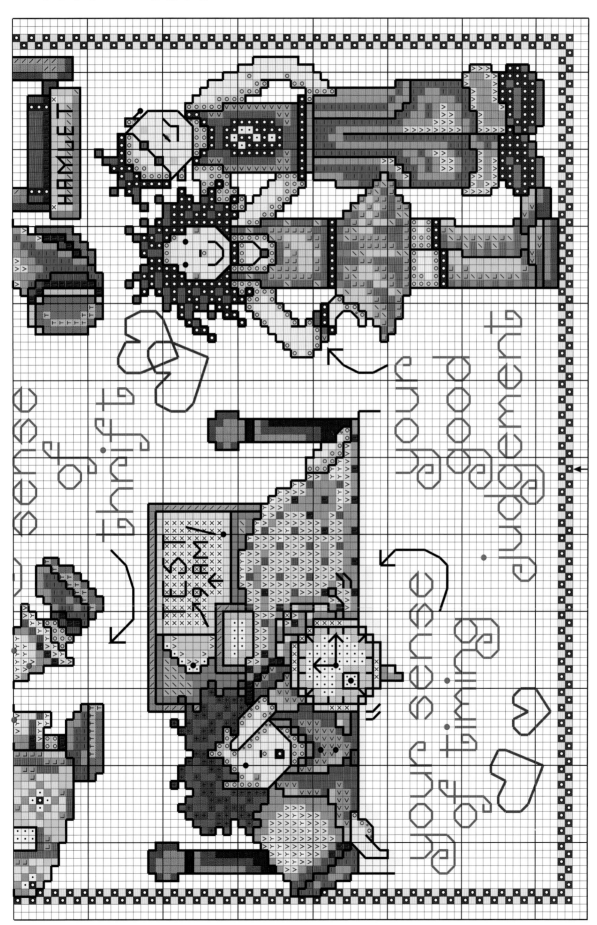

Backstitch
310
311
552
817

French knots
310
311
350
725

HAMLET

your sense of thrift

your good judgement

your sense of timing

Our Anniversary

Enduring love is a precious gift and always a cause for celebration. An anniversary is a time to reflect on years past and also to share visions of the future. Love's promise is that as each day together goes by, difficulties shared are eased and happiness shared is doubled. This anniversary sampler speaks of the wisdom and power of abiding love. Made up as a luxurious photo album or scrapbook, it provides a beautiful home to hold wonderful memories of a full life together. Stitch the charming card to tuck into an anniversary gift. Newly wed or in your golden years together, when you know you have found that special person, surely the best is yet to be.

Anniversary Album

Stitch count
131h x 105w

Design size
23.8 x 19cm (9½ x 7½in)

Materials

38 x 33cm (15 x 13in) antique white 28-count Monaco evenweave

Tapestry needle size 24

DMC stranded cotton (floss) as listed in chart key

Lightweight iron-on interfacing

One standard three-ring photo album 29.2 x 25.5cm (11½ x 10in)

0.5m (½yd) white cotton batting or felt

0.5m (½yd) fabric for outside cover and 0.5m (½yd) fabric for inside covers to tone with embroidery

Two pieces 28 x 24cm (11 x 9½in) heavy white card

1.25m (1¼yd) decorative lace, 0.5m (½yd) ribbon and a satin rose

Spray craft adhesive and permanent fabric glue

1 Prepare for work, referring to page 101 if necessary. Mark the centre of the fabric and centre of the chart on pages 52–53. Mount your fabric in an embroidery frame if you wish.

2 Start stitching from the centre of the chart and fabric, working over two fabric threads and using two strands of stranded cotton (floss) for all cross stitches. Work all French knots using two strands wound once around the needle. Following the chart colours, use one strand for all backstitches. Use the alphabet on page 51 to stitch names and anniversary dates. Plan the letters on graph paper first to ensure they fit the space.

3 Once all the stitching is complete, make up a covered photo album as follows. Cut a piece of iron-on interfacing 2.5cm (1in) larger than the finished embroidery all around. With the wrong side of your work facing, centre the interfacing and fuse it to the embroidery. Trim the embroidery ten rows beyond the design.

4 Open the photo album binder and lay it flat on the batting or felt. Trace the outline of the album on to the batting or felt and cut out. In a well-ventilated area, spray one outside cover of the album with spray adhesive. Attach the batting or felt and repeat the process for the spine and back cover. Do not pull the felt over the cover too tightly and ensure that the album will close. Trim the edges flush. (Instructions continue overleaf.)

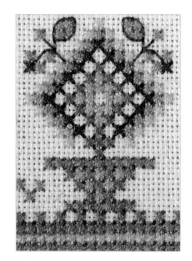

Loves
Promise

is fulfilled
one day at a time
one year to the next
one joy
after another

RICHARD
and
ELLEN

1982

2007

*True love begins
in a moment,
grows over time,
and lasts for
eternity.*

5 Lay the open album on the outer cover fabric. Measure and mark 5cm (2in) from all edges and cut the fabric. From the same fabric, cut two strips the length of the metal spine and 7.6cm (3in) wide. Fold over 6mm (¼in) on one long edge of each strip and press. Spray glue on the back of each strip and slide the folded edge under each side of the metal spine. You can use a butter knife to help push the edge beneath the spine.

6 Using the fabric for the inside cover, cut two pieces 2.5cm (1in) larger than the card all around. Spray glue on one side of each piece of the cut card. Place the fabric on the glued card leaving 2.5cm (1in) of fabric all around. Turn the edges to the back of the card and glue using permanent fabric glue.

7 Centre the open album on the outside cover fabric. Turn all the edges to the inside and glue, starting with the centre of each edge, leaving the corners and 7.6cm (3in) from the spine free. Carefully ease the corners to fit and then glue. At the top and bottom edges by the spine measure the fabric 1.25cm (½in) away from the fold in the album towards the outer edge and clip within 1.25cm (½in) of the top edge. Fold the fabric under, between the two cuts, and tuck the folded edge behind the top edge of the metal spine and glue in place.

8 To assemble the album, cut the ribbon in half and centre one piece on each opening edge of the album at least 5cm (2in) in towards the centre. Glue in place. Carefully glue the back of the covered card close to the edge. Centre and attach this to the inside covers making sure that the fold on the inside of the album is free to close.

9 Centre the finished embroidery on the cover and glue in place, taking care that no glue oozes out from the sides. Draw a thin bead of fabric glue around the edge of the embroidery starting and ending at centre bottom and attach the decorative lace. Hide the ends of the lace by gluing on a satin rose.

Anniversary Card
Stitch count 71h x 45w
Design size 10 x 6.4cm (4 x 2½in)

Work the design on a 23 x 20.3cm (9 x 8in) piece of antique white 18-count Aida, using the chart opposite. Use two strands of stranded cotton for cross stitch and one for backstitch. Once complete, mount your work in a suitable card (see page 102).

Anniversary Card
DMC stranded cotton
Cross stitch

- 501
- 502
- 503
- 832
- 834
- T 3363
- 3364
- 3688
- o 3689
- 3803

Backstitch
— 3051

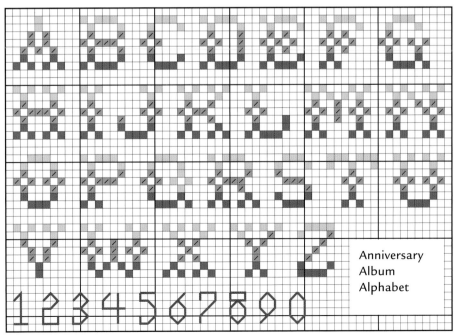

Anniversary
Album
Alphabet

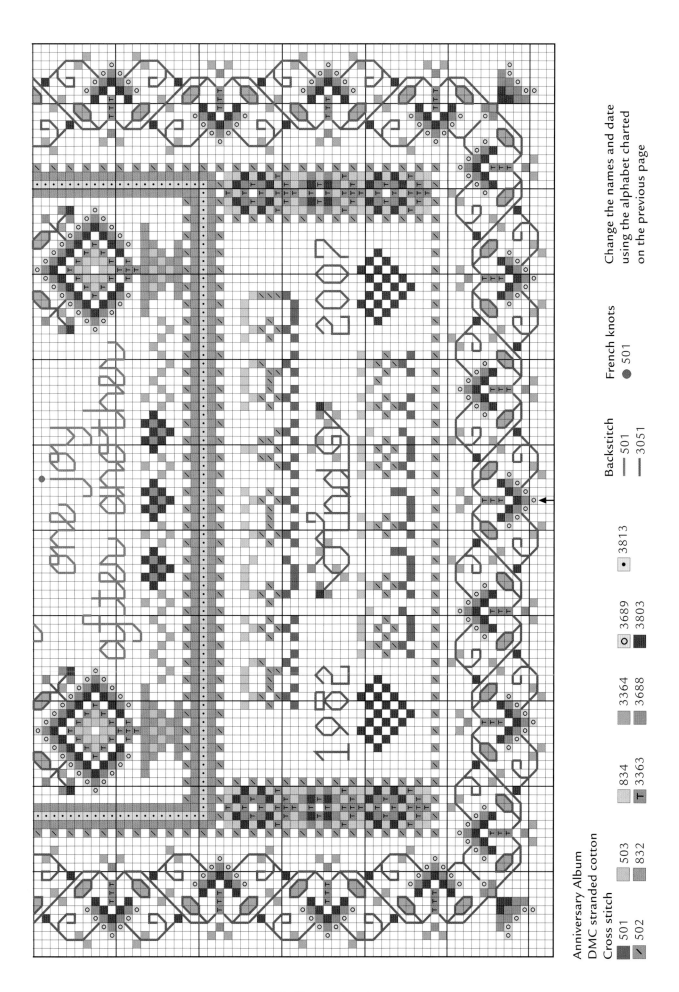

Anniversary Album
DMC stranded cotton
Cross stitch

| | 501 | | 503 |
| | 502 | | 832 |

| | 834 | T | 3363 |
| | | | 3364 |

| | 3689 | O | |
| | 3688 | | 3803 |

| • | 3813 |

Backstitch
— 501
— 3051

French knots
● 501

Change the names and date using the alphabet charted on the previous page

Eastern Promise

The decorative arts of India are rich in tradition and dazzling in inspiration. In this land of philosophy and spirituality, symbolic motifs decorated everyday items treasured for generations. As art and life become one, religion and social customs freely intertwine. In ancient Hindu Sanskrit words, this sampler beseeches us to recognize each glorious day as a promise of happiness past, present and future. Arabesque leaves and striking paisleys add a graceful flow to the design. It can be stitched as a whole or parts of it selected for attractive smaller projects, as shown on the following pages.

Eastern Promise Sampler

Stitch count
225h x 169w

Design size
41 x 31cm (16 x 12in)

Materials

53.5 x 43cm (21 x 17in) antique white 14-count Aida

Tapestry needle size 24 and a beading needle

DMC stranded cotton (floss) as listed in chart key

Kreinik #4 Very Fine Braid: 202HL Aztec gold

Mill Hill Magnifica™ glass beads: 10010 royal pearl and 10091 gold nugget

1 Prepare for work, referring to page 101 if necessary. Mark the centre of the fabric and centre of the chart on pages 60–63. Mount your fabric in an embroidery frame if you wish.

2 Start stitching from the centre of the chart and fabric, using two strands of stranded cotton (floss) for full and three-quarter cross stitches. Work French knots using one strand wound twice around the needle. Use one strand to stitch all Kreinik cross stitches and backstitches. Work all other backstitches with one strand.

3 Using a beading needle and matching thread, attach the beads (see page 102) according to the positions shown on the chart.

4 Once the stitching is complete, finish your picture by mounting and framing (see page 103).

Fruit Card
Stitch count 41h x 41w
Design size 6.5 x 6.5cm (2½ x 2½in)

Mounted in a golden card to send a lovely message of thanks, this motif of bountiful fruits reflects the abundance and glory of a spiritual life. Stitch the fruit motif from the main chart on a 19cm (7½in) square of antique white 16-count Aida following the stitching instructions for the main sampler above. Mount the finished embroidery in a suitable card (see page 102) and embellish with a ribbon bow.

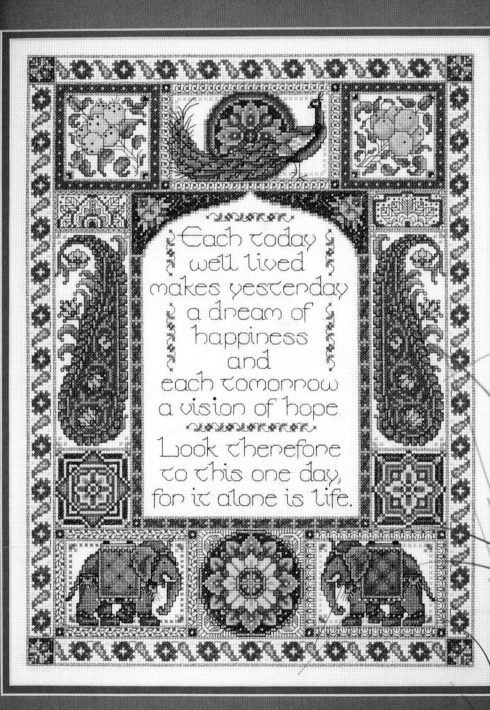

Each today
well lived
makes yesterday
a dream of
happiness
and
each tomorrow
a vision of hope.
Look therefore
to this one day,
for it alone is life.

Peacock Sachet

Made up as a sweet-scented sachet, this brilliant peacock represents beauty and immortality and would make a wonderful gift for an admired friend.

Stitch count
41h x 69w

Design size
7.5 x 12.5cm (3 x 5in)

Materials

20.5 x 25.5cm (8 x 10in) antique white 14-count Aida

Tapestry needle size 24 and a beading needle

DMC stranded cotton (floss) as listed in chart key

Kreinik #4 Very Fine Braid: 202HL Aztec gold

Mill Hill Magnifica™ glass beads: 10010 royal pearl and 10091 gold nugget

Lightweight iron-on interfacing

0.25m (¼yd) fabric for backing

Polyester filling or pot-pourri

61cm (24in) length of decorative braid and one button

Permanent fabric glue

1 Prepare for work. Mark the centre of the fabric and the centre of the charted motif and start stitching from the centre following the stitching instructions for steps 2 and 3 of the sampler on page 54.

2 Make up into a sachet as follows. Trim the embroidery twelve rows beyond the design. Cut iron-on interfacing to the same size and press on to the wrong side of the embroidery. Cut the backing fabric to the same size as the trimmed embroidery and pin in place, right sides facing. With matching sewing thread stitch a 1.25cm (½in) seam all around, leaving an opening at the bottom edge. Turn through to the right side and stuff with polyester filling or pot-pourri.

3 Attach the decorative cord by slipstitching or gluing it around all the edges of the sachet, beginning and ending at centre bottom. Tuck the cord ends inside the sachet and slipstitch closed. To finish off, attach a decorative button at the centre bottom.

The peacock's tail, emblazoned with hundreds of iridescent all-seeing eyes, made this bird a messenger of the gods.

Paisley Bookmark

The henna motifs known as Mehndi and a rhythmic paisley in radiant colours embellish a delightful gift for your favourite reader. Use the paisley motif from the main chart.

Stitch count
111h x 30w

Design size
17.5 x 4.8cm (7 x 1⁷⁄₈in)

Materials
30.5 x 18cm (12 x 7in) antique white 16-count Aida

❋

Tapestry needle size 24 and a beading needle

❋

DMC stranded cotton (floss) as listed in chart key

❋

Kreinik #4 Very Fine Braid: 202HL Aztec gold

❋

Mill Hill Magnifica™ glass beads: 10091 gold nugget

❋

18 x 5cm (7 x 2in) fusible web

❋

18 x 5cm (7 x 2in) white felt for backing

1 Prepare for work. Mark the centre of the fabric and the centre of the charted motif – note that the henna motif is repeated below the paisley pattern. Start stitching from the centre of the fabric following the stitching instructions for steps 2 and 3 of the sampler on page 54.

2 Once the stitching is complete, trim the embroidery eight rows beyond the edges of the design. To create a fringe, run a machine stitch around all four edges, three rows beyond the embroidery. Carefully pull out the threads up to the stitching line. Cut a piece of fusible web and a piece of felt to the size of the finished design area. Place the web on the back of the design area, layer the felt on top of the web and iron to fuse according to the manufacturer's instructions.

On the Earth, there is no better treasure than kindness; no better wealth than contentment.

Lotus Mandala Bowl

Indian artisans were hugely inspired by the world around them and this small lotus medallion from the main chart turns a trinket bowl into something quite special.

Stitch count
41h x 41w

Design size
5.8 x 5.8cm (2¼ x 2¼in)

Materials

17.8 x 17.8cm (7 x 7in) antique white 18-count Aida

Tapestry needle size 24 and a beading needle

DMC stranded cotton (floss) as listed in chart key

Kreinik #4 Very Fine Braid: 202HL Aztec gold

Mill Hill Magnifica™ glass beads: 10010 royal pearl and 10091 gold nugget

Wooden trinket bowl (see Suppliers)

36cm (14in) length of decorative braid

One decorative button

Permanent fabric glue

1 Prepare for work, referring to page 101 if necessary. Mark the centre of the fabric and the centre of the charted motif.

2 Start stitching from the centre of the charted motif and fabric, using two strands of stranded cotton (floss) for cross stitches. Work French knots using one strand wound twice around the needle. Use one strand to stitch all Kreinik cross stitches and backstitches. Work all other backstitches with one strand.

3 Using a beading needle and matching thread, carefully attach the beads (see page 102) according to the positions shown on the chart.

4 Once all the stitching is complete, mount in the bowl lid according to the manufacturer's instructions. Glue the decorative braid around the outer rim of the pot lid, starting and ending at centre bottom. Attach a button where the ends of the braid meet to hide the join.

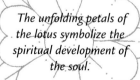

The unfolding petals of the lotus symbolize the spiritual development of the soul.

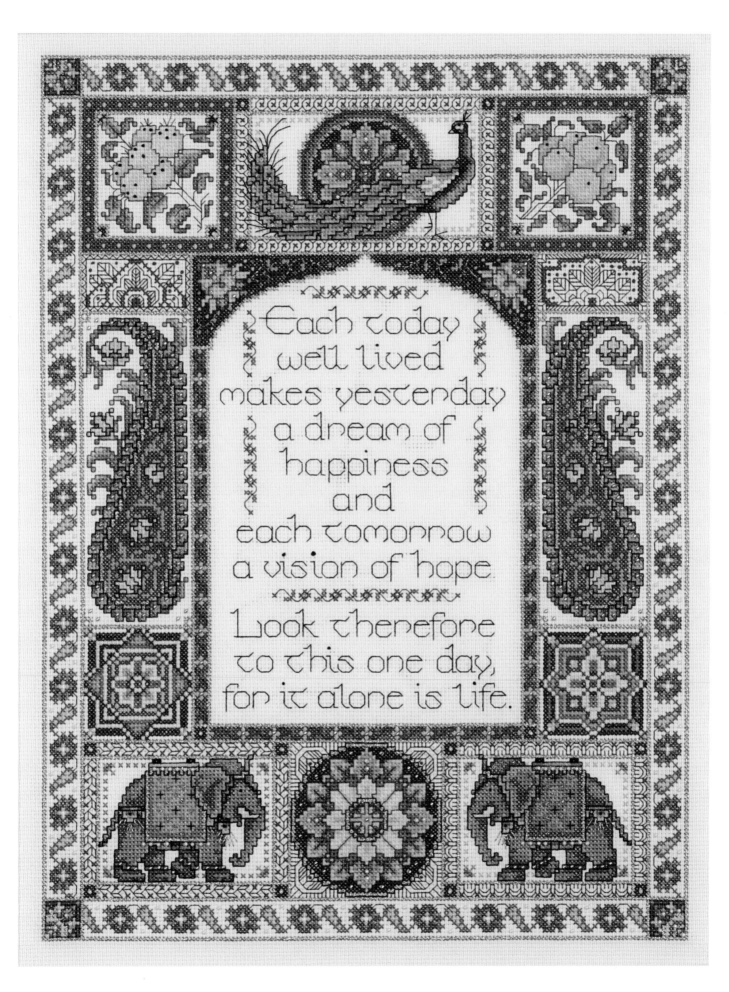

Eastern Promise
DMC stranded cotton
Cross stitch

	322
	349
✓	351
	471
✗	472
	601
○	603
	605
	741
+	742
	743
	744
	803
V	975
I	992
	993
L	3023
	3022
–	3346
	3371
Y	3753
T	3755
	3787
	3814
•	blanc
	Kreinik #4 braid 202HL Aztec gold (1 strand)

Backstitch
— 975
— 3345
— 3371
— Kreinik #4 braid 202HL Aztec gold

French knots
● 975
● 3371
● Kreinik #4 braid 202HL Aztec gold

Mill Hill
Magnifica beads
◉ 10010 royal pearl

◉ 10091 gold nugget

orrow

of hope.

erefore

ne day,

e is life.

Eastern Promise
DMC stranded cotton
Cross stitch

	322
	349
/	351
	471
✕	472
	601
○	603
	605
	741
+	742
	743
	744
	803
V	975
I	992
	993
L	3023
	3022
−	3346
	3371
Y	3753
T	3755
	3787
	3814
•	blanc
	Kreinik #4 braid 202HL Aztec gold (1 strand)

Backstitch
—— 975
—— 3345
—— 3371
—— Kreinik #4 braid 202HL Aztec gold

French knots
● 975
● 3371
● Kreinik #4 braid 202HL Aztec gold

Mill Hill
Magnifica beads
◐ 10010 royal pearl

◯ 10091 gold nugget

Children's Blessings

Rocking gently on a soft blue sea, an ark filled with all creatures great and small cheerfully announces the arrival of the newest addition to the family. Cuddly pandas, baby bluebirds and mischievous mice share the top deck with friendly giraffes who keep a lookout over the menagerie. The bumblebees buzz with excitement while cavorting monkeys, tigers, penguins and butterflies are all a-twitter with the happy news.

As well as making this irresistible sampler you could preserve photos of baby's homecoming and important milestones with a delightful design for a little photo album (overleaf). There's a fun card too that is quick to stitch, the perfect finish to a trio of special gifts that baby's parents are sure to treasure.

Birth Sampler

Stitch count
182h x 138w

Design size
33 x 25cm (13 x 10in)

Materials

46 x 38cm (18 x 15in) antique white
28-count evenweave

Tapestry needle size 24

DMC stranded cotton (floss)
as listed in chart key

1 Prepare for work, referring to page 101 if necessary. Mark the centre of the fabric and centre of the chart on pages 68–71. Mount fabric in an embroidery frame if you wish.

2 Start stitching from the centre of the chart, working over two fabric threads and using two strands of stranded cotton (floss) for full and three-quarter cross stitches. Following the colour changes on the chart, use one strand for backstitches and one strand wrapped twice around the needle for French knots. Use the alphabet on page 67 to stitch baby's name and birth date. Plan the letters on graph paper first to ensure they fit the space.

3 Once all stitching is complete, finish your sampler by mounting and framing (see page 103).

Baby Card
Stitch count 49h x 49w
Design size 9 x 9cm (3½ x 3½in)

Three baby animals join together to wish a special blessing for baby in this delightful card design. Stitch it on a 21.5cm (8½in) square of antique white 14-count Aida following the chart and key on page 67. Work full and three-quarter cross stitches with two strands of stranded cotton and backstitch with one. Work French knots using one strand wound twice around the needle. Mount the finished embroidery in a suitable card (see page 102) and embellish with a ribbon bow.

Bluebird Photo Album

Two sweet bluebirds surrounded by blossoms and butterflies adorn the cover of this little album. You could attach this design to a store-bought album or make up a covered album of your own with the instructions provided on page 103.

Stitch count
59h x 47w

Design size
10.7 x 8.5cm (4¼ x 3½in)

Materials

23 x 21.5cm (9 x 8½in) antique white 14-count Aida

Tapestry needle size 24

DMC stranded cotton (floss) as listed in chart key

Lightweight iron-on interfacing

51cm (20in) length of decorative trimming

One small button

1 Prepare for work. Mark the centre of the fabric and centre of the chart opposite. Start stitching from the centre of the chart, using two strands of stranded cotton (floss) for full and three-quarter cross stitches. Following the colour changes on the chart, use one strand for backstitches and one strand wrapped twice around the needle for French knots.

2 Trim the finished embroidery to five rows beyond the design.

Cut a piece of iron-on interfacing the size of the trimmed embroidery and fuse to the wrong side according to the manufacturer's instructions. Attach the finished embroidery to the front of a purchased album using double-sided tape or make up your own cloth-covered album (see page 103). Edge the embroidery by gluing on the decorative trim, beginning and ending at centre bottom and attaching a decorative button where the ends meet.

It is not a slight thing when they, who are so fresh from God, love us.
(Charles Dickens)

Baby Card

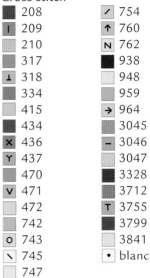

Baby Card and Photo Album
DMC stranded cotton
Cross stitch

▨	208	∕	754
I	209	↑	760
	210	N	762
	317	▉	938
⊥	318		948
	334		959
	415	→	964
	434		3045
✕	436	–	3046
Y	437		3047
	470		3328
V	471		3712
	472	T	3755
	742		3799
O	743		3841
∖	745	•	blanc
	747		

Backstitch
— 938
— 3328

French knots
● 938 (alphabet)
● 3799

Photo Album

Birth Sampler Alphabet

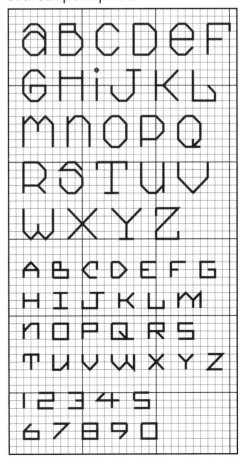

Birth Sampler
DMC stranded cotton
Cross stitch

■	208
I	209
	210
	317
⊥	318
	334
	415
	434
X	436
Y	437
	470
V	471
	472
	742
O	743
\	745
	747
L	754
↑	760
N	762
+	801
■	938
	948
	959
→	964
–	3045
	3046
	3047
	3328
	3712
T	3755
	3799
/	3841
•	blanc

Backstitch

—	334
—	938
—	3328

French knots
● 938
● 3799

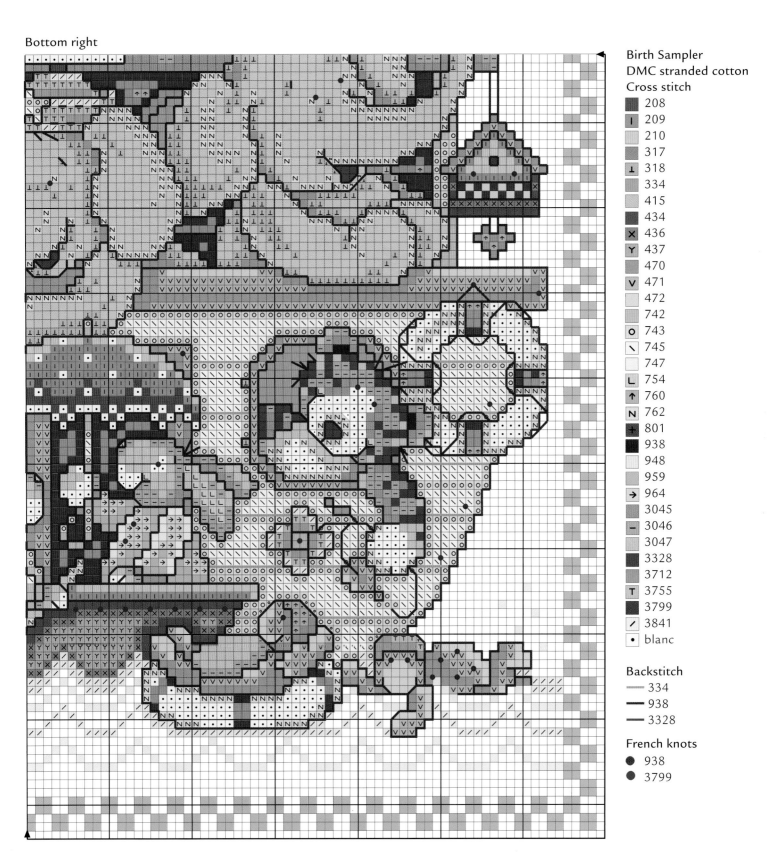

Birth Sampler
DMC stranded cotton
Cross stitch

■	208
I	209
	210
	317
⊥	318
	334
	415
	434
✗	436
Y	437
	470
V	471
	472
	742
O	743
\	745
	747
L	754
↑	760
N	762
✛	801
■	938
	948
	959
→	964
	3045
–	3046
	3047
	3328
	3712
T	3755
	3799
/	3841
•	blanc

Backstitch
—— 334
—— 938
—— 3328

French knots
● 938
● 3799

Joys of Gardening

Gardeners are a special breed and have a philosophy all their own. A passion near and dear to my heart, I know how the hours drift by unnoticed while digging, planting, and pruning. From this intense avocation have come many words of wisdom exclusive to this happy lot. These notices illustrate some of the phases of maintaining the perfect garden. Join the club and get a scoop on 'the best dirt' with your gardening friends. Wish everyone a wonderful life with a shower of wildflowers. Present your favourite lawn-mowing man with words that speak to the woes of weekly lawn maintenance, reminding him that humour will lighten the load. For a gardening chum who is lucky enough to be retiring, there's a playful card to help her indulge her obsession. We all understand after all, that what we need in life comes down to just three things – 'eat, sleep, and garden'.

Gardening Notices

Stitch count (each notice)
99h x 71w

Design size (each notice)
18 x 13cm (7 x 5in)

Materials (each notice)
30.5 x 25.5cm (12 x 10in) Fiddler's Light 14-count Aida

Tapestry needle size 24

DMC stranded cotton (floss) as listed in chart key

You know you are a real gardener when you think compost is a fascinating subject.

1 Prepare for work, referring to page 101 if necessary. Mark the centre of the fabric and centre of the chart (pages 76–79). Mount fabric in an embroidery frame if you wish.

2 Start stitching from the centre of the chart and fabric, using two strands of stranded cotton (floss) for full and three-quarter cross stitches. Work all French knots using two strands wound once around the needle. Use two strands for the white backstitches in the 'Life is Simple' notice (chart on page 78). Following the chart colours, use one strand for all other backstitches and for long stitches.

3 Once all the stitching is complete, finish your picture by mounting and framing (see page 103).

Retirement Card

This fun card hints at some of the joys of retirement – gardening, gardening and more gardening! You could also work the design over one block of 14-count Aida and stitch it on the front of a gardening apron.

Stitch count
65h x 65w

Design size
9.2 x 9.2cm (3½ x 3½in)

Materials
23 x 23cm (9 x 9in) Fiddler's Light
18-count Aida

Tapestry needle size 24

DMC stranded cotton (floss)
as listed in chart key

1 Prepare for work, referring to page 101 if necessary. Mark the centre of the fabric and the centre of the chart opposite. Mount fabric in an embroidery frame if you wish.

2 Start stitching from the centre of the chart and centre of the fabric, using two strands of stranded cotton (floss) for full and three-quarter cross stitches. Work

all French knots using two strands wound once around the needle. Following the chart colours use one strand for all backstitches and any long stitches.

3 Once all the stitching is complete, mount your embroidery in a suitable card (see page 102 and also suggestions for decorating card mounts).

This design would also look lovely made up as a gardening journal cover, see page 96 for instructions.

RETIREMENT
MEANS A
FULL-TIME
COMMITMENT
♡ TO ♡
GARDENING

Retirement Card
DMC stranded cotton

Cross stitch

▪ 310	351	∧ 743	✕ 945
312	415	744	951
+ 318	⊙ 603	✕ 869	3755
– 334	676	905	3829
349	L 729	╱ 906	• blanc
V 350	742	907	

Backstitch/Long stitch
— 310
— 349
— 905

French knots
● 310
◉ 743

I Fought the Lawn
DMC stranded cotton
Cross stitch

- 310
- 312
- 317
- 318
- 334
- 349
- 350
- 351
- 415
- 434
- 435
- 604
- 676
- 729
- 742
- 743
- 744
- 801
- 869
- 904
- 905
- 906
- 907
- 945
- 951
- 3755
- 3829
- blanc

Backstitch/
Long stitch
— 310
— 905

French knots
● 310

Gardeners Know
the Best Dirt
DMC stranded cotton
Cross stitch

■	208
←	209
	210
◉	310
■	312
■	317
+	318
−	334
	415
N	434
⌐	435
ı	602
O	603
	604
	676
L	729
	742
∧	743
	744
■	801
＼	869
Y	904
	905
∕	906
	907
X	945
	951
T	3325
	3755
	3829
•	blanc

Backstitch/
Long stitch
—— 310
—— 905

French knots
● 209
● 310
○ blanc

Life is Simple
Eat, Sleep, Garden
DMC stranded cotton
Cross stitch

▨	310
▨	317
+	318
–	334
▨	349
V	350
▨	351
I	602
o	603
▨	604
▨	676
L	729
∧	742
▨	743
▨	744
▨	869
Y	904
/	905
▨	906
▨	907
×	945
▨	951
T	3325
▨	3755
▨	3829
•	blanc

Backstitch/
Long stitch

— 310
— 349
▭ blanc (2 strands)

French knots
● 310
○ blanc

May All Your
Weeds be Wildflowers
DMC stranded cotton
Cross stitch

■	208
←	209
	210
▨	310
▨	317
+	318
−	334
▌	602
O	603
	604
L	729
	742
∧	743
	744
╲	869
	905
╱	906
	907
✕	945
	951
▨	3755
	3829
•	blanc

Backstitch/
Long stitch
—— 310
—— 905

French knots
● 310
● 905

Christmas Crackers

I t's a jolly time all through the house when Santa is scheduled to arrive. Candles glow, lights twinkle, anticipation grows and the spirit of the season is upon us. Merry Christmas banners remind Santa to be sure to stop, while a pile of jubilant snowmen gather to declare, 'We believe!' Tuck a small present into a Happy Christmas gift bag or make a scented sachet bag adorned with a joyful snowman. Beads and metallic threads add sparkle to four ornaments easily worked on plastic canvas. Two little pillow ornaments, complete with brightly coloured hanging cords, are edged in shimmering red and green beads. Spread the joy and deck the halls!

Let it Snow Card
Stitch count 37h x 37w
Design size 6.7 x 6.7cm (2½ x 2½in)

This card features one of the pillow ornament designs (chart on page 88). These designs are sized to fit in a large square card mount and this card has been worked on 28-count light blue Jubilee evenweave (Zweigart code 501). Follow steps 1 and 2 of the stitching instructions on page 84. Mount the embroidery into your card (see page 102) and add your own festive touch with a gold pen and cheery red bow.

Christmas Banners

These two bright and cheerful banners are great fun and are sure to add a colourful touch to your Christmas décor. See page 80 for a picture of the second banner.

Stitch count (each banner)
111h x 63w

Design size (each banner)
20 x 11.5cm (8 x 4½in)

Materials (each banner)
33 x 25.5cm (13 x 10in) Fiddler's Light 14-count Aida

Tapestry needle size 24 and a beading needle

DMC stranded cotton (floss) as listed in chart key

Kreinik #4 Very Fine Braid: 028 citron

Mill Hill glass seed beads: 00557 gold

23 x 15.2cm (9 x 6in) piece of red or green felt for backing

Lightweight interfacing and fusible web

One tassel to tone with embroidery

Permanent fabric glue

30.5cm (12in) length of 6mm (¼in) wide red ribbon

12.7cm (5in) green wooden bell pull (see Suppliers)

Teddies and snowmen, a time of good cheer. Could that be Santa's footsteps we hear?

1 Prepare for work. Mark the centre of the fabric and chart (pages 86 and 87). Use an embroidery frame if you wish.

2 Start stitching from the centre of the chart and fabric. Use one strand for Kreinik cross stitches and two strands of stranded cotton (floss) for all other full and three-quarter cross stitches. Work all French knots using two strands wound once around the needle. Use one strand for backstitches. Use two strands of DMC 816 for backstitch lettering 'Santa Stop Here' and two strands of DMC 700 for 'We Believe'. Using a beading needle and matching thread, attach the beads.

3 Make up a banner as follows. Draw a pencil cutting line along the sides and bottom edges ten rows beyond the design. Draw a line 5.7cm (2¼in) beyond the top edge of the embroidery. Place lightweight interfacing on the back of the embroidery and fuse according to the manufacturer's instructions. Cut the shape along the pencil lines.

4 Fold the sides and bottom edges to the back leaving four rows beyond the embroidery and making a point at the bottom. Press and glue. Fold the top raw edge under by six rows, press and glue in place. Fold back the top of the banner, leaving nine rows showing and press. Cut the felt backing and fusible web 6mm (¼in) smaller than the banner's shape.

Sandwich the web between the wrong side of the embroidery and the felt, tucking both under the top fold-over. Press to fuse. Stitch a small stitch where the folded edge meets the back of the banner.

5 Put the bell pull dowel through the fold. Cut the ribbon in half and attach it to the bell pull by making a loop and gluing each end in place. Make a hanging bow. Make a tassel from matching floss (see page 103) or buy a tassel and attach it to the bottom of the banner.

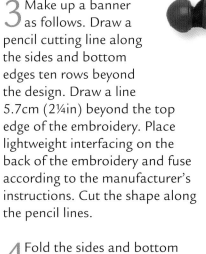

Gift Bags

These pretty bags are very simple to stitch and make up and can be filled with seasonal pot-pourri or a little gift. See page 81 for a picture of the second bag.

Stitch count (each bag)
55h x 33w

Design size (each bag)
10 x 6cm (4 x 2½in)

Materials (each bag)
Snow Place Like Home: 23 x 20.3cm (9 x 8in) light blue Jobelan 28-count evenweave (Wichelt code 42921)

Happy Christmas: 23 x 20.3cm (9 x 8in) putty 28-count Cashel Linen (Zweigart code 345)

Tapestry needle size 24

DMC stranded cotton (floss) as listed in chart key

Kreinik #4 Very Fine Braid: 028 citron

Two pieces fabric 25.4 x 15.2cm (10 x 6in) for bag

Lightweight interfacing and fusible web

0.5m (½yd) narrow red ribbon

1 Prepare for work, referring to page 101 if necessary. Mark the centre of the fabric and centre of the chart (page 88). Mount fabric in an embroidery frame if you wish.

2 Start stitching from the centre of the chart and fabric, stitching over two threads. Use one strand for Kreinik thread cross stitches and two strands of stranded cotton (floss) for all other full and three-quarter cross stitches. Work all French knots using two strands wound once around the needle. Following the chart colours, use one strand for all backstitches.

3 Once all the stitching is complete, trim the finished embroidery ten fabric threads beyond the design. Create a fringe by machine stitching in toning thread four rows beyond the embroidery all around. Pull out the threads up to the stitching line. Cut lightweight interfacing and fusible web the size of the embroidery up to where the fringe starts. Fuse the interfacing to the back of the design.

4 Make a bag by placing the two bag fabric pieces right sides together. Stitch a 1.25cm (½in) seam down each long side and across the

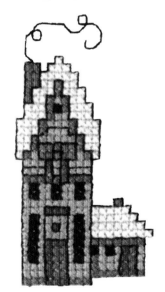

bottom leaving the top open. Trim the corners and press seams open. Turn the bag to the right side. Fold under 6mm (¼in) along the top raw edge to the wrong side and stitch in place. Turn this finished edge towards the inside of the bag by 1.25cm (½in) Press in place and stitch down to secure.

5 Place the fusible web beneath the finished embroidery and centre it on the bag, leaving 1.25cm (½in) at the bottom edge. Fuse according to the manufacturer's instructions. Insert some fragrant Christmas pot-pourri or a small gift. Tie the length of ribbon at the top to gather it closed.

Pillow Ornaments

These sweet ornaments are perfect quick-stitch Christmas gifts, given an extra sparkle with an edging of glass beads. See page 80 for a picture of the second pillow.

Stitch count (each pillow)
37h x 37w

Design size (each pillow)
6.7 x 6.7cm (2½ x 2½in)

Materials (each pillow)

Be Jolly: two pieces 25.5 x 25.5cm (10 x 10in) antique blue 28-count Jobelan evenweave (Wichelt code 42936)

Let it Snow: two pieces 25.5 x 25.5cm (10 x 10in) platinum 28-count Cashel linen (Zweigart code 770)

Tapestry needle size 24 and a beading needle

DMC stranded cotton (floss) as listed in chart key

Kreinik #4 Very Fine Braid: 028 citron

Be Jolly: Mill Hill glass seed beads: 00165 Christmas red

Let it Snow: Mill Hill glass seed beads: 02055 brilliant green

Polyester stuffing

17.8cm (7in) decorative cord for hanging

1 Prepare for work, referring to page 101 if necessary. Mark the centre of the fabric and centre of the chart (page 88). Mount fabric in an embroidery frame if you wish.

2 Start stitching from the centre of the chart and fabric, stitching over two threads. Use one strand for Kreinik thread cross stitches and two strands of stranded cotton (floss) for all other full and three-quarter cross stitches. Work all French knots using two strands wound once around the needle. Following the chart colours, use one strand for all backstitches.

3 Once the stitching is complete, make up into a pillow ornament. Using one strand of stranded cotton (floss) DMC 349 for 'Be Jolly' and DMC 700 for 'Let it Snow', stitch a running stitch two fabric

threads beyond the last row of the embroidery, making the pillow 39 x 39 stitches. Repeat this running stitch around a 39 x 39 stitch area on the blank fabric.

4 Trim both pieces of fabric to within four rows of the running stitch and fold along this line of stitches. Finger press in place, mitring the corners neatly. With wrong sides together, use two strands of matching stranded cotton to whip stitch the running backstitches from both pieces, starting at centre bottom. As you go, add a matching seed bead to every other stitch. Before finishing, stuff with a little polyester filling. Finish whip stitching until all edges are sealed. Attach the decorative cord to each top corner with a small tacking (basting) stitch and fray the edges into little tassels.

Trim the tree with lights and holly, Christmas time is here. Fill the room with songs so jolly, and loved ones oh so dear.

Tree Ornaments

These charming ornaments are worked on rigid plastic canvas and embellished with sparkling beads, making them perfect for decorating the tree or as special gift tags.

Stitch count (maximum)
51h x 43w

Design size
9.3 x 7.8cm (3½ x 3in)

Materials

(for all four ornaments)

20 x 28cm (8 x 11in) sheet of white 14-count plastic canvas

Tapestry needle size 24 and a beading needle

DMC stranded cotton (floss) as listed in chart keys

Mill Hill glass seed beads: 00165 Christmas red; 00557 gold and 02055 brilliant green

Lightweight iron-on interfacing

20 x 28cm (8 x 11in) white felt for backing

Permanent fabric glue

1m (1yd) decorative cord (for hanging)

1 Prepare the plastic canvas by trimming any rough edges. You should be able to stitch all ornaments on a single sheet. Plan carefully, allowing at least two bars between designs. Following the chart on page 89, use one strand for Kreinik thread cross stitches and two strands of stranded cotton (floss) for all other cross stitches. Work French knots using two strands wound once around the needle. Following the chart colours, use one strand for all backstitches. Using a beading needle and matching thread, attach the beads (see page 102).

2 Once stitching is complete cut iron-on interfacing to cover all the ornaments and, using a press cloth on top, fuse to the back of the canvas according to the manufacturer's instructions. Carefully cut out each finished ornament leaving one row of canvas around the design. Cut a piece of felt backing roughly the shape of each ornament and glue to the backs. Glue only the backs of the stitched ornaments and stay within the edges of the embroidery. Trim the felt backing as necessary so it doesn't show on the front.

3 Thread a 23cm (9in) length of cord through the edge of the top centre of the ornament. To finish, tie ends in a secure knot to create a hanging loop.

Christmas Banners
DMC stranded cotton
Cross stitch
▨	318
◉	349
▨	350
T	415
▨	700
╱	702
▨	703
−	725
▨	726
V	741
▨	742
▨	747
+	762
▨	797
╲	798
▨	799
▨	817
▨	869
▨	963
I	3045
▨	3046
×	3716
◈	310
•	blanc
▨	Kreinik #4 braid 028 citron (1 strand)

Backstitch
—	310
—	700
—	816
—	817
▬	Kreinik #4 braid 028 citron (1 strand)

French knots
●	310
●	700
●	817
○	blanc

Mill Hill beads
◉	00557 gold

We Believe

Happy Christmas

Snow Place Like Home

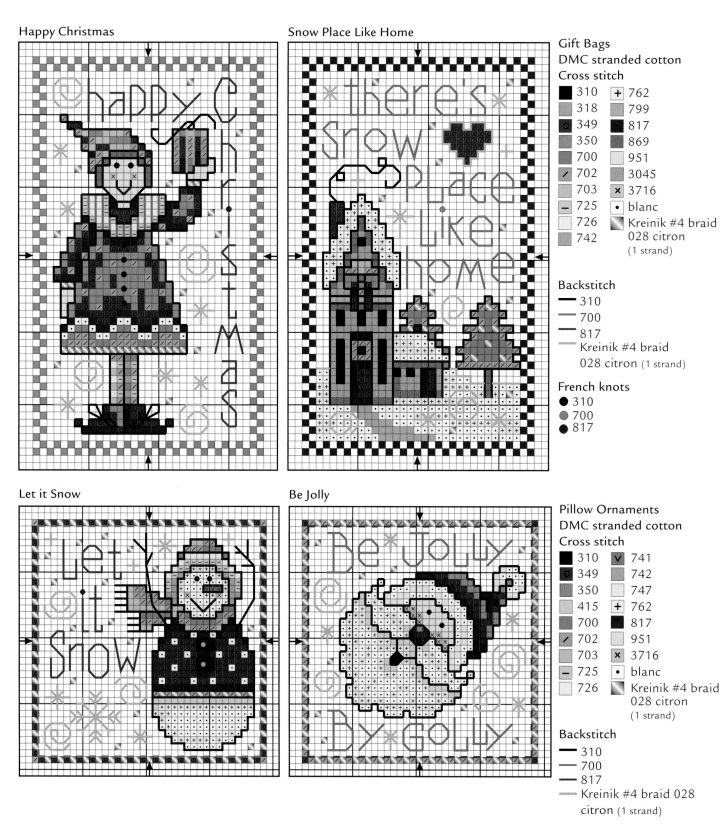

Let it Snow

Be Jolly

Gift Bags
DMC stranded cotton
Cross stitch

■	310	+	762
▦	318		799
◉	349	■	817
▦	350		869
▦	700		951
╱	702		3045
	703	✕	3716
−	725	•	blanc
	726	▨	Kreinik #4 braid
	742		028 citron
			(1 strand)

Backstitch
— 310
— 700
— 817
Kreinik #4 braid
028 citron (1 strand)

French knots
● 310
● 700
● 817

Pillow Ornaments
DMC stranded cotton
Cross stitch

■	310	⌵	741
◉	349		742
▦	350		747
	415	+	762
▦	700	■	817
╱	702		951
	703	✕	3716
−	725	•	blanc
	726	▨	Kreinik #4 braid
			028 citron
			(1 strand)

Backstitch
— 310
— 700
— 817
Kreinik #4 braid 028
citron (1 strand)

French knots
● 310
● 817
● Kreinik #4 braid 028
citron (1 strand)

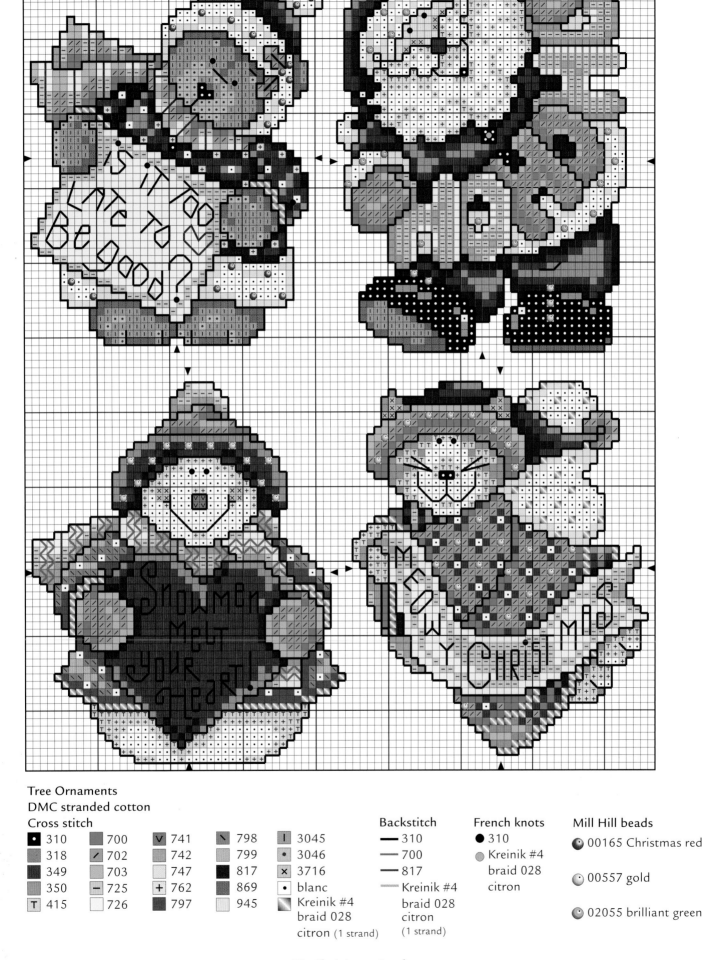

Tree Ornaments

DMC stranded cotton

Cross stitch

● 310	▨ 700	▾ 741	▨ 798	▮ 3045	
318	╱ 702	742	799	● 3046	
349	703	747	747	✕ 3716	
350	− 725	+ 762	817	● blanc	
T 415	726	797	869	▨ Kreinik #4	
			945	braid 028	
				citron (1 strand)	

Backstitch
— 310
— 700
— 817
▨ Kreinik #4
braid 028
citron
(1 strand)

French knots
● 310
● Kreinik #4
braid 028
citron

Mill Hill beads
● 00165 Christmas red
● 00557 gold
● 02055 brilliant green

89 Christmas Crackers

Family Sentiments

It is said that a family is a circle of love: here we not only find comfort and support but also a loving environment in which to grow and blossom. In our day-to-day lives we don't often take the time to let each other know just how precious this circle of love really is. Let mother know that her love brings sunshine to your heart with a sweet trinket box edged in lace. Dad can proudly display a sign praising all that he means to you. For grandma, there is a perfumed sachet to tell her she has a heart of gold. Grandpa will tell stories and show off the grandkids in a handsome photo case. There is nothing like a sister, a forever friend, so treat her to a pretty bag for jewellery. For your brother, make up a leather journal to record his latest adventures. The designs can also be made into gift cards for special occasions.

Heart of Gold Card
Stitch count 43h x 67w
Design size 7.8 x 12.2cm (3 x 4¾in)

Each design in this chapter is sized to fit in a standard rectangular card mount. Using the chart on page 98, this card has been worked on a 20.3 x 25.5cm (8 x 10in) piece of 28-count antique white evenweave. Follow steps 1 and 2 of the sachet instructions on page 95. Mount the embroidery into your card (see page 102) for a heartfelt personal gift that Grandma is sure to cherish.

MY **DAD**
KEEPS HIS PROMISES
DRIES MY TEARS
MAKES ME SMILE
FILLS MY LIFE WITH
LOVE

MY
GRANDPA
TELLS ME STORIES
TEACHES ME WISDOM
TICKLES MY HEART

A Father's Promise

Send words of praise and love to your dad with this stylish little hanging.

Stitch count
43h x 67w

Design size
7.8 x 12.2cm (3 x 4¾in)

Materials

20.3 x 25.4cm (8 x 10in) white
14-count Aida

Tapestry needle size 24

DMC stranded cotton (floss)
as listed in chart key

9 x 13.3cm (3½ x 5¼in)
heavy white card

Two pieces of felt 15.2 x 19.6cm
(6 x 7¾in) to tone with embroidery

Lightweight iron-on interfacing
and fusible web

0.5m (½yd) length of 6mm (¼in)
wide ribbon to tone

50.8cm (20in) length of decorative
braid to tone

Permanent fabric glue

Three decorative buttons

1 Prepare for work. Mark the centre of the fabric and centre of the chart on page 99.

2 Start stitching from the centre of the chart and fabric, using two strands of stranded cotton (floss) for cross stitches. Work French knots using two strands wound once around the needle. Use one strand for backstitches (and any long stitches).

3 Make up into a hanging as follows. Cut iron-on interfacing 2.5cm (1in) larger than the finished embroidery all around. With the wrong side of your work facing, centre the interfacing and fuse to the embroidery. Trim the embroidery ten rows beyond the design. Fold edges to the back leaving a three-row border all around. Press the folds. Trim the heavy card to fit behind the embroidery under the folded edges. Glue the edges to the back of the card with permanent fabric glue.

4 Cut a piece of fusible web to match the felt size and sandwich between the two pieces of felt. Use a press cloth and iron to fuse the layers, leaving the top long edge open. Use pinking shears all around the felt close to the edge. Cut the length of ribbon in half and position the two lengths 4cm (1½in) from either side of the felt, inserting it 2.5cm (1in) between the layers. Iron to fuse the top edge.

5 Apply permanent fabric glue sparingly to the back of the embroidery close to the edge. Position the embroidery on the felt, with an equal border all around, making sure no glue oozes out. Glue the decorative braid along the folded edge of the embroidery, starting and ending at centre bottom. Add a button at bottom centre and where the ribbon meets the top edge. To finish, tie the ribbons in a bow for a hanger.

*A father is someone
you look up to
no matter how tall
you grow.*

A Mother's Love

This charming keepsake box is made even more special by the addition of a pretty trim and satin rose.

Stitch count

67h x 43w

Design size

12.2 x 7.8cm (4¾ x 3in)

Materials

25.5 x 20.3cm (10 x 8in) white
14-count Aida

❊

Tapestry needle size 24

❊

DMC stranded cotton (floss)
as listed in chart key

❊

Lightweight iron-on interfacing

❊

50.8cm (20in) decorative trim

❊

One small satin rose

❊

Permanent fabric glue

❊

Covered box about 15.2 x 14cm
(6 x 5½in) (from stationery
and craft shops)

1 Prepare for work. Mark the centre of the fabric and centre of the chart on page 100.

2 Start stitching from the centre of the chart and fabric, using two strands of stranded cotton (floss) for cross stitches. Work French knots using two strands wound once around the needle. Use two strands for DMC 164 backstitches and one strand for other backstitches.

3 Mount on the box top as follows. Cut iron-on interfacing 2.5cm (1in) larger than the design all around. With the wrong side of your work facing, centre the interfacing and fuse to the embroidery. Trim the embroidery four rows beyond the design.

4 Apply glue to the back of the embroidery close to the edges, centre it on the top of the box and adhere. Glue the decorative trim along the raw edge of the embroidery starting and ending at centre bottom. To finish, attach the satin rose where the trim ends meet.

Mothers hold their children's hands for a while, and their hearts forever.

Grandpa's Wisdom

This attractive photo case made from faux suede is very easy to make up and perfect to send words of love to your grandpa.

Stitch count
43h x 67w

Design size
7.8 x 12.2cm (3 x 4¾in)

Materials

20.3 x 25.5cm (8 x 10in) white 14-count Aida

❄

Tapestry needle size 24

❄

DMC stranded cotton (floss) as listed in chart key

❄

20.3 x 46cm (8 x 18in) Ultrasuede® to tone with embroidery for backing

❄

Lightweight iron-on interfacing and fusible web

❄

51cm (20in) length of decorative cord to tone

❄

30.5cm (12in) of 6mm (¼in) wide ribbon to tone

❄

One small button

❄

Permanent fabric glue

❄

10 x 15.2cm (4 x 6in) ready-made photo pages (from stationery and craft shops)

1 Prepare for work. Mark the centre of the fabric and centre of the chart on page 98. Use an embroidery frame if you wish.

2 Follow the stitching instructions in step 2 on page 92.

3 Make up the photo case as follows. Cut iron-on interfacing 2.5cm (1in) larger all round than the embroidery and fuse to the back. Trim the embroidery to within five rows of the stitched border.

4 Fold the piece of Ultrasuede® in half lengthways and press to crease. Lay the fabric flat, fold the two ends towards the centre crease by 10cm (4in) and tack (baste) in place. Stitch the unfolded edges together using contrasting sewing thread. Use pinking shears to pink the sewn sides close to the edge.

5 Fold the stitched case in half, pockets on the inside. Cut a piece of fusible web the size of the trimmed embroidery. Centre the embroidery on the outside of the folded case, sandwiching the web between the case and the wrong side of the embroidery. Press to fuse. Using a thin line of fabric glue, attach the decorative cord around the edge of the embroidery, beginning and ending at centre bottom. Cut the satin ribbon in half and glue it to the case where the cord ends meet, attaching a small button to hide raw ends. At the centre of the back edge, attach the other half of the ribbon by turning over 1.25cm (½in) and gluing in place. To finish, slip the photo pages into the inside pockets of the case and tie the ribbons together.

A grandpa is a little bit parent, a little bit teacher and a little bit best friend.

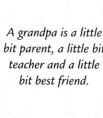

Grandma's Heart of Gold

This pretty little sachet pillow, embellished with a heart charm, is sure to show grandma just how much you love her. The design is shown as a card on page 90.

Stitch count
43h x 67w

Design size
7.8 x 12.2cm (3 x 4¾in)

Materials
20.3 x 25.5cm (8 x 10in) white 14-count Aida

Tapestry needle size 24

DMC stranded cotton (floss) as listed in chart key

Kreinik #4 Very Fine Braid: 028 citron

17.8 x 17.8cm (7 x 7in) backing fabric

Lightweight iron-on interfacing

1m (1yd) decorative cord to tone with embroidery

Polyester filling

Permanent fabric glue

One decorative gold heart charm

1 Prepare for work. Mark the centre of the fabric and centre of the chart on page 98. Use an embroidery frame if you wish.

2 Follow the stitching instructions in step 2 on page 92.

3 Make up into a sachet pillow as follows. Cut iron-on interfacing 2.5cm (1in) larger than the embroidery all around. With the wrong side facing, centre the interfacing and fuse to the embroidery. Trim the embroidery twelve rows beyond the design.

4 To create a hanging loop, cut a 23cm (9in) length of decorative cord and place the ends 3.8cm (1½in) from either side of the embroidery, matching raw edges with the top edge of the trimmed

embroidery. Cut the backing fabric to the same size as the trimmed embroidery, right sides facing, and pin in place. Using matching sewing thread, stitch a 1.25cm (½in) seam all around, leaving an opening at the bottom edge. Turn through to the right side and stuff with polyester filling.

5 Attach the decorative cord by gluing it around all edges, beginning and ending at centre bottom. Tuck the cord in at the centre bottom and slipstitch closed. To finish off, attach the heart charm at the centre bottom of the pillow.

Grandmas never run out of hugs or cookies.

World's Best Brother

There are many smart journals like this available in various stores, perfect for adding a heartfelt cross stitch sentiment.

Stitch count
67h x 43w

Design size
12.2 x 7.8cm (4¾ x 3in)

Materials
25.4 x 20.3cm (10 x 8in) white
14-count Aida
❄
Tapestry needle size 24
❄
DMC stranded cotton (floss)
as listed in chart key
❄
Lightweight iron-on interfacing
❄
1m (1yd) length of 2.5cm (1in) wide
ribbon to tone with embroidery
❄
Permanent fabric glue
❄
19 x 13.3cm (7½ x 5¼in) leather
journal (available at stationers)

*This design can also
be mounted on felt for
a cheerful hanging as
on page 92.*

1 Prepare for work. Mark the centre of the fabric and centre of the chart on page 100. Use an embroidery frame if you wish.

2 Follow the stitching instructions in step 2 on page 92.

3 Make up the journal as follows. Cut iron-on interfacing 2.5cm (1in) larger than the embroidery all around. With the wrong side of your work facing, centre the interfacing and fuse to the embroidery. Trim the embroidery four rows beyond the design.

4 Centre the embroidery on the journal cover and attach using permanent fabric glue. Cut the ribbon into four pieces, measuring to match the embroidery sides and adding 1.25cm (½in) to each length. Glue ribbon strips one row away from the edge of the stitching, overlapping and turning under the cut ends. Glue a strip of the remaining ribbon to the binding of the book for a nice finish.

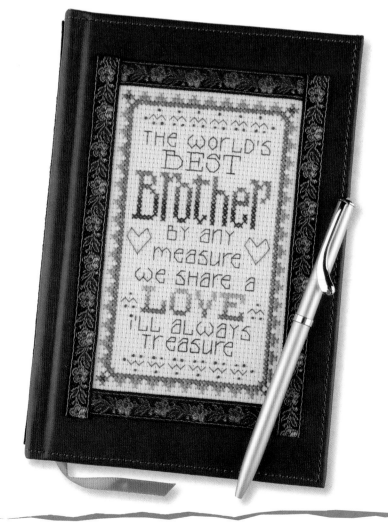

Forever Sisters

With its loving message, your sister is sure to treasure this adorable drawstring bag. Choose her favourite colour for the bag fabric.

Stitch count
43h x 67w

Design size
7.8 x 12.2cm (3 x 4¾in)

Materials
20.3 x 25.5cm (8 x 10in) white
14-count Aida

Tapestry needle size 24

DMC stranded cotton (floss)
as listed in chart key

Two pieces of fabric 30.5 x 23cm
(12 x 9in) for the bag

Lightweight iron-on interfacing
and fusible web

50.8cm (20in) length of
decorative trim

Three small satin roses

Permanent fabric glue

1m (1yd) of 1cm (⅜in) wide ribbon
to tone with embroidery

*A sister knows
everything about you
. . . and loves you
anyway!*

1 Prepare for work. Mark the centre of the fabric and centre of the chart on page 99. Use an embroidery frame if you wish.

2 Follow the stitching instructions in step 2 on page 92.

3 Make up into a drawstring bag as follows. Cut iron-on interfacing 2.5cm (1in) larger than the embroidery all around. With the wrong side facing, centre the interfacing and fuse to the embroidery. Trim the embroidery four rows beyond the design.

4 Make the bag by placing the bag fabric pieces right sides together. Leaving 14cm (5½in) open at the top on both sides, stitch a 1.25cm (½in) seam along the bottom and up both sides. Trim the bottom corners diagonally and press seams open. Turn the bag to the right side. Finish the raw edge by turning it over 6mm (¼in), then press and stitch close to the edge. Turn the top of the bag to the inside about 9cm (3½in) to make a hem

and channel for the drawstring and press. Stitch a line 3.2cm (1¼in) from the folded edge and another 1.25cm (½in) below that.

5 Cut fusible web the same size as the prepared embroidery. Place the embroidery 2.5cm (1in) from the bottom and sides of the bag with the web behind it and fuse according to the manufacturer's instructions. Glue the decorative trim along the raw edge of the embroidery starting and ending at centre bottom and attaching a satin rose where the ends meet.

6 Thread the length of ribbon through the casing for a drawstring and attach a small rose at each end. To finish, pull the ribbons to gather and tie in a bow.

MY GRANDPA TELLS ME STORIES TEACHES ME WISDOM TICKLES MY HEART

MY GRANDMA HAS A HEART OF GOLD

Grandpa and Grandm
DMC stranded cotton
Cross stitch

▓	208
╱	209
░	211
◉	310
▓	312
L	322
░	334
▬	350
T	471
•	745
▓	817
▓	906
▓	972
░	993
▓	3687
O	3688
∧	3803

Backstitch

▬	312
▬	817
▬	3345
▬	Kreinik #4 braid 028 citron

French knots

●	312
●	817

Dad and Sister
DMC stranded cotton
Cross stitch

- 208
- 310
- 312
- 322
- 334
- 350
- 725
- 817
- 906
- 907
- 961
- 962
- 3831

Backstitch
- 310
- 312
- 975
- 3345
- 3831

French knots
- 208
- 310
- 312
- 975

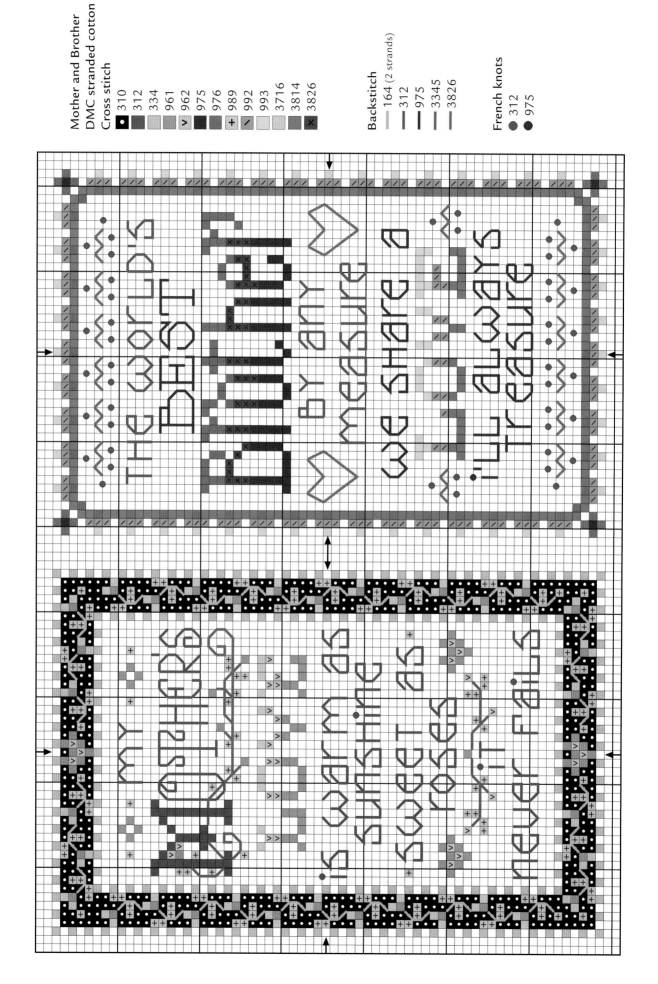

Useful Information

This section describes the materials and equipment required, the basic techniques and stitches used and some general making up methods. Refer to Suppliers for useful addresses.

Materials

Fabrics

The designs have been worked mostly on a blockweave fabric called Aida. If you change the gauge (count) of the material, that is the number of holes per inch, then the size of the finished work will alter accordingly. Some of the designs have been stitched on evenweave and in this case need to be worked over two fabric threads instead of one block. The photo frame on page 20 and the tree ornaments on page 85 were worked on plastic canvas.

Threads

The projects have been stitched with DMC stranded embroidery cotton (floss) but you could match the colours to other thread ranges – ask at your local needlework store. The six-stranded skeins can easily be split into separate strands. The project instructions tell you how many strands to use. Some projects use a Kreinik metallic thread for added glitter – use one strand for this thread.

Needles

Tapestry needles, available in different sizes, are used for cross stitch as they have a rounded point and do not snag fabric. You will need a thinner beading needle to attach the small glass seed beads used in some of the projects.

Frames

It is a matter of personal preference as to whether you use an embroidery frame to keep your fabric taut while stitching. Generally speaking, working with a frame helps to keep the tension even and prevent distortion, while working without a frame is faster and less cumbersome. There are various types on the market – look in your local needlework store for some examples.

Techniques

Preparing the Fabric

Before starting work, check the design size given with each project and make sure that this is the size you require for your finished embroidery. Your fabric should be at least 5cm (2in) larger all the way round than the finished size of the stitching, to allow for making up. Before beginning to stitch, neaten the fabric edges either by hemming or zigzagging to prevent fraying as you work. If using plastic canvas, neaten all the edges by trimming off any sharp or rough pieces.

Finding the Fabric Centre

Marking the centre of the fabric is important regardless of which direction you work from, in order to stitch the design centrally on the fabric. To find the centre, fold the fabric in half horizontally and then vertically, then tack (baste) along the folds (or use tailor's chalk). The centre point is where the two lines of tacking (basting) meet. This point on the fabric should correspond to the centre point on the chart. Remove these lines on completion of the work.

Calculating Design Size

Each project gives the stitch count and finished design size but if you want to work the design on a different count fabric you will need to re-calculate the finished size. Count the number of stitches in each direction on the chart and then divide these numbers by the fabric count number, e.g., 140 x 140 ÷ 14-count = a design size of 10 x 10in (25.5 x 25.5cm). Working on evenweave usually means working over two fabric threads, so divide the fabric count by two before you start calculating.

Using Charts and Keys

The charts in this book are easy to work from. Each square represents one stitch. Each coloured square, or coloured square with a symbol, represents a thread colour, with the code number given in the chart key. A few of the designs use fractional stitches (three-quarter stitches) to give more definition. Solid coloured lines show where backstitches or long stitches are to be worked. French knots are shown by coloured circles. Larger coloured circles with a dot indicate beads.

Each complete chart has arrows at the side to show the centre point, which you could mark with a pen. Where the charts have been split over several pages, the key is repeated. For your own use, you could colour photocopy and enlarge charts, taping the parts together.

Starting and Finishing Stitching

Avoid using knots when starting and finishing as this will make your work uneven and lumpy when mounted. Instead, bring the needle up at the start of the first stitch, leaving a 'tail' of about 2.5cm (1in) at the back. Secure this tail by working the first few stitches over it. Start new threads by first passing the needle through several stitches on the back of the work.

To finish off thread, pass the needle through several nearby stitches on the wrong side of the work, then cut the thread off, close to the fabric.

Washing and Pressing

If you need to wash your finished embroidery, first make sure the stranded cottons are colourfast by washing them in tepid water and mild soap. Rinse well and lay out flat to dry completely before stitching. Wash completed embroideries in the same way. To iron embroidery, use a medium setting, covering the ironing board with a thick layer of towelling. Place the stitching right side down and press gently, taking extra care with glass seed beads and metallic threads.

The Stitches

Backstitch

Backstitches are used to give definition to parts of a design and to outline areas. Many of the charts use different coloured backstitches. Follow Fig 1, bringing the needle up at 1 and down at 2. Then bring the needle up again at 3 and down at 4, and so on.

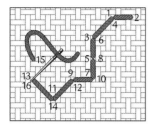

Fig 1 Working backstitch

Cross Stitch

A cross stitch can be worked singly (Fig 2a) or a number of half stitches can be sewn in a line and completed on the return journey (Fig 2b).

To make a cross stitch over one block of Aida, bring the needle up through the fabric at the bottom left side of the stitch (number 1 on Fig 2a) and cross diagonally to the top right corner (2). Push the needle through the hole and bring up through the bottom right corner (3), crossing the fabric diagonally to the top left corner to finish the stitch (4). To work the next stitch, come up through the bottom right corner of the first stitch and repeat the sequence.

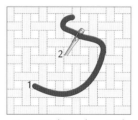

Fig 2a Working a single cross stitch

To work a line of cross stitches, stitch the first part of the stitch as above and repeat these half cross stitches along the row. Complete the crosses on the way back. Note: for neat work, always finish the cross stitch with the top stitches lying in the same diagonal direction.

Fig 2b Working cross stitch in two journeys

French Knot

French knots have been used as eye highlights and details in some of the designs, in various colours. To work, follow Fig 3, bringing the needle and thread up through the fabric at the exact place where the knot is to be positioned. Wrap the thread once or twice around the needle (according to the project instructions), holding the thread firmly close to the needle, then twist the needle back through the fabric as close as possible to where it first emerged. Holding the knot down carefully, pull the thread through to the back leaving the knot on the surface, securing it with one small stitch on the back.

Fig 3 Working a French knot

Long Stitch

This is used for stars and whiskers in some of the projects. Simply work a long, straight stitch (Fig 4) starting and finishing at the points indicated on the chart.

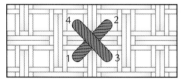

Fig 4 Working a long stitch

Three-quarter Cross Stitch

Three-quarter cross stitches give more detail to a design and can create the illusion of curves. They are shown by a triangle within a square on the charts. Working three-quarter cross stitches is easier on evenweave fabric than Aida (see Fig 5). To work on Aida, make a quarter stitch from the corner into the centre of the Aida square, piercing the fabric, and then work a half cross stitch across the other diagonal.

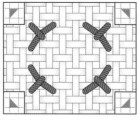

Fig 5 Working three-quarter cross stitch

Attaching Beads

Adding beads will bring sparkle and texture to your cross stitch embroidery. Attach seed beads using ordinary sewing thread that matches the fabric colour and a beading needle or very fine 'sharp' needle and a half or whole cross stitch (Fig 6).

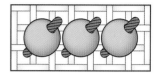

Fig 6 Attaching beads

Making Up

The embroideries from this book are very versatile and have been made up in many ways. Generally, making up is included with projects but some general techniques are described here.

Making Up into a Card

Many of the designs or parts of larger designs can be stitched and made up into cards. You will need: a ready-made card mount (aperture to fit embroidery) and craft glue or double-sided tape.

Trim the edges of the embroidery to fit the card. Apply a thin coat of glue or a piece of double-sided tape to the inside of the card opening. (Note: some cards already have this tape in place.) Position the embroidery, checking that the stitching is central, and press down firmly. Fold the spare flap inside, sticking in place with glue or tape, and leave to dry before closing.

You can easily add a personal touch to ready-made card mounts by gluing on ribbons, bows, beads, buttons, stickers or personal doodles in waterproof markers. Visit your local stationery or craft store and explore all the possibilities.

Making Up as a Framed Picture

Many of the designs in this book make wonderful framed pictures. You will need: a picture frame (aperture size to fit embroidery); a piece of plywood or heavyweight card slightly smaller than the frame and adhesive tape or a staple gun.

Iron your embroidery and trim the edges if necessary, then centre the embroidery on the plywood or thick card. Fold the edges of the embroidery to the back and use adhesive tape or a staple gun to fix in place. Insert the picture into the frame and secure with adhesive tape or staples. For a polished finish, with a wider choice of mounts and frames, take your work to a professional framer.

Making a Tassel

Cut a piece of stiff card, about 1.5cm (½in) longer than the desired size of the tassel. Choose a thread colour to match your project and wrap it around the card to the desired thickness. Slip a length of thread through the top of the tassel and tie in a knot. Slide the threads off the card. Bind the top third of the tassel with length of thread and then trim the tassel ends .

Covering an Album

These are general instructions for creating your own fabric-covered albums, like the small bluebird photo album shown in the Children's Blessings chapter.

Materials

One three-ring photo album sized to suit your project

0.5m (½yd) fabric for outside cover to tone with embroidery

0.5m (½yd) fabric for inside covers to tone with embroidery

0.5m (½yd) white cotton wadding (batting) or felt

Two 25 x 30cm (10 x 12in) pieces of heavy white card

1m (1yd) decorative trim to tone with embroidery

0.5m (½yd) decorative 1cm (⅜in) ribbon to tone with embroidery

Spray glue and permanent fabric glue

One decorative button

1 Measure the inside cover of the album to the fold just before the metal spine. Cut two pieces of heavy card to the measurements, less 1.25cm (½in). Open the binder and lay it flat on the wadding (batting) or felt. Trace the outline of the album on to the batting or felt and cut out. In a well-ventilated area, spray one outside cover of the album with spray glue. Attach the batting or felt and repeat the process for the spine and back cover. Do not pull the felt over the cover too tightly, making sure that the album will close. Trim the edges flush.

2 Lay the open album on the outer cover fabric. Measure and mark 5cm (2in) from all edges and cut the fabric. From the same fabric, cut two strips measuring the length of the metal spine plus 7.5cm (3in) wide. Fold over 6mm (¼in) on one long edge of each strip and press. Spray glue on the back of each strip and slide the folded edge under each side of the metal spine. You can use a butter knife to help push the edge beneath the spine.

3 Using the fabric for the inside cover, cut two pieces 2.5cm (1in) larger than the card. Spray glue on one side of each piece of cut card. Centre the card over the fabric. Turn the edges to the back of the card and glue with permanent fabric glue.

4 Centre the open album on the outside cover fabric. Turn all the edges to the inside and glue, starting with the centre of each edge, leaving the corners and 7.5cm (3in) from the spine free. Carefully ease the corners to fit, and glue. At the top and bottom edges by the spine measure the fabric 1.25cm (½in) away from the fold in the album on each side of the metal spine and clip within 1.25cm (½in) of the top edge. Fold the fabric under between the two cuts and then tuck the folded edge behind the top edge of the metal spine.

5 To assemble the album, cut the ribbon in half and centre one piece on each opening edge of the album at least 5cm (2in) in towards the centre. Glue the back of the covered card. Centre and attach this to the inside covers, making sure that the fold on the inside of the album is free for closing.

6 Centre the finished embroidery on the cover and glue in place, taking care that no glue oozes out from the sides. Draw a thin bead of fabric glue around the edge of the embroidery starting and ending at centre bottom and attach the decorative trim. To finish, glue on a decorative button where the ends meet.

Acknowledgments

With love and an abundance of thanks to every one of the wonderful women that have stitched the models for this book: Judi Trochimiak, Rindy Richards, Lisa Rabon, Helen McClain, Lynda Moss, MaryAnn Stephens, Bev Ritter, Lois Schultz, Meem Breyer, Lori West, Debbie Fitzgerald and Belinda Barnhart. I cherish you all and admire your dedication and incredible abilities.

This is my fifth book for David & Charles and I am so very happy to be able to continue my work with all the wonderful people there. Many thanks to Jennifer Fox-Proverbs and Bethany Dymond for keeping things flowing smoothly, to Pru Rogers and Charly Bailey for their excellent book design, and to Kim Sayer for the fine photography. Heartfelt thanks to Cheryl Brown, my commissioning editor, whose insights, understanding and enthusiasm are more than any designer could hope for, and to Rona Boyne for all the wonderful input she has provided during the designing process. Lastly, my affection and appreciation go out to my editor, Lin Clements, whom I was finally able to meet in person last year. Only her marvellous spirit supersedes her many talents.

Suppliers

Charles Craft Inc
PO Box 1049, Laurenburg, NC 28353, USA
tel: 910 844 3521
email: ccraft@carolina.net
www.charlescraft.com
For fabrics for cross stitch including Fiddler's Light Aida and Monaco evenweave and many useful pre-finished items (Coats Crafts UK supply some Charles Craft products in the UK)

Coats Crafts UK
PO Box 22, Lingfield Estate, McMullen Road, Darlington, County Durham DL1 1YQ, UK
tel: 01325 365457 (for a list of stockists)
For Anchor stranded cotton (floss) and other embroidery supplies. Coats also supplies some Charles Craft products

Design Works Crafts Inc
170 Wilbur Place, Bohemia, New York 11716, USA
tel: 631 244 5749 fax: 631 244 6138
email:
customerservice@designworkscrafts.com
For cross stitch kits featuring designs by Joan Elliott

DMC Creative World
Pullman Road, Wigston, Leicestershire LE18 2DY, UK
tel: 0116 281 1040 fax: 0116 281 3592
www.dmc/cw.com
For stranded cotton (floss) and other embroidery supplies

Joan Elliott
www.joanelliottdesign.com

Framecraft Miniatures Ltd
Unit 3, Isis House, Lindon Road, Brownhills, Walsall, West Midlands, WS8 7BW, UK
tel: 01543 360842
www.framecraft.com
USA Distributor: Anne Brinkley Designs, Inc 3895B N Oracle Rd, Tuscon, AZ 85705, USA
tel: 520 888 1462 fax: 520 888 1483
For wooden trinket bowls and boxes, notebook covers, pincushions, and many pre-finished items with cross stitch inserts, including the trinket bowl, code W3R

Impress Cards & Craft Materials
Slough Farm, Westhall, Halesworth, Suffolk, IPN19 8RN, UK
tel: 01986 781422 fax: 01986 781677
email: sales@impresscards.co.uk
www.impresscards.com
For card mounts and finishing accessories, including the large square card mount, code 48 and large rectangle card mount, code 42

Kreinik Manufacturing Company, Inc
1708 Gihon Road, Parkersburg, WV 26102, USA
tel: 1 800 5372166 fax: (304) 4284326
email: information@kreinik.com
For a wide range of metallic threads, blending filaments and metallic cords

Madeira Threads (UK) Ltd
PO Box 6, Thirsk, North Yorkshire YO7 3YX, UK

tel: 01845 524880
email: info@madeira.co.uk
www.madeira.co.uk
For Madeira stranded cotton (floss) and other embroidery supplies

Market Square (Warminster) Ltd
Wing Farm, Longbridge Deverill, Warminster, Wiltshire BA12 7DD, UK
tel: 01985 841041 fax: 01985 541042
For work boxes and trinket boxes

Sudberry House
12 Colton Road, East Lyme, CT 06333 USA
tel: 860 739 6951
email: sales@sudberry.com
www.sudberry.com
For quality wooden products for displaying needlework, including the Simply Square wooden box, code 99721

Wichelt Imports
N162 Hwy 35, Stoddard, WI 54658, USA
tel: 800 356 9516 fax: 608 788 6040
www.wichelt.com
For Mill Hill beads, Jobelan evenweave and other cross stitch fabrics, wooden bell pulls, buttons and accessories

Zweigart/Joan Toggit Ltd
262 Old Brunswick Road, Suite E, Piscataway, NJ 08854-3756 USA
tel: 732 562 8888
email: info@zweigart.com
www.zweigart.com
For a large selection of cross stitch fabrics including Cashel Linen® and Jubilee®

Index